SUNBATHiNG iN SiBERiA:

A Marriage of East and West
in Post-Soviet Russia

Michael Oliver-Semenov was born in Ely, Cardiff, but now resides in central Siberia. Since ditching his career as a banking clerk in 1997 he has published words and poetry in a plethora of magazines, anthologies and journals worldwide, including *Blown*, *The Morning Star*, *Orbis*, *Ten of the Best*, *Wales Arts Review*, *Mandala Review* and *Ink Sweat and Tears*. He divides his time between growing vegetables at his family dacha, teaching English and writing for *The Siberian Times*. http://thepoetmao.webs.com

SUNBATHING IN SIBERIA:

A Marriage of East and West in Post-Soviet Russia

M.A. Oliver-Semenov

PARTHIAN

Parthian
The Old Surgery
Napier Street
Cardigan
SA43 1ED

www.parthianbooks.com

First published in 2014
© M.A. Oliver-Semenov 2014
All Rights Reserved

ISBN 978-1-908946744

Editor: Susie Wild
Cover design by Torben Schacht
Typeset by Elaine Sharples
Printed and bound by Gomer Press, Llandysul, Wales

Published with the financial support of the Welsh
Books Council

To everyone living in Russia,
everyone living outside of Russia,
and everyone in-between.

CONTENTS:

PART 1

Aeroflot Flight SU0242.
March 29th 2011. London — Moscow

Jaffa Cake: A round soft sponge type thing topped with orange coloured jelly and covered in a thin layer of chocolate. How was anyone supposed to know a Jaffa is an orange when it doesn't say so on the box? It said 'Jaffa Cakes', meaning that Jaffa was either the name of the company or it was an actual fruit in its own right, like a kiwi or a banana. Or it could have even been a totally made-up name like rock cakes, which to my knowledge contain no rocks at all. How was I supposed to know that Jaffa wasn't a country, or a person? Where I grew up there was a local man called Jaffa; and although I suspected it wasn't his real name it was the only name anyone knew him by; and besides, people had all sorts of weird names, especially in the food world, like Captain Birdseye and Mr Kipling. It was a basic logical deduction that led me to believe that, much in the same way Mr Kipling had invented a type of cake, Jaffa Cakes were invented by someone named Jaffa.

I was in my late twenties when I discovered that this wasn't true, that Jaffa was, in fact, a type of orange from a place named Jaffa. I listened to my friends talking about some poor bugger who had admitted that he didn't know what a Jaffa was. And to my newly acquired middle class, it was something they could laugh heartily about. They couldn't imagine living in a world where people had no experience of Jaffa oranges being anything other than a slice of gooey jelly placed on top of a cake that came in packs of twelve and was nice enough, and affordable enough, that your mother bought a pack every Friday when she did the shopping.

Why is a Jaffa Cake a Jaffa Cake and not an orange cake anyway? An apple pie is just an apple pie. It's not as if a pie baked with Cox's apples is called a Cox Pie, or a Golden Delicious Pie or Pink Lady Pie. Why not orange cake? Because Jaffa sounds posher, I guessed. Though the only Jaffa I ever knew was the fella' who apparently, back in 1985, could get you cheap tracksuits that 'fell off the back of a lorry'. Took me a while to figure out what that one meant too. For many years I wondered why they didn't just make lorries with better locks or load them with less stuff before they travelled.

This was, of course, a distraction. It was all I could think of to keep myself from going crazy. As I took the last of the Jaffa Cakes from the box in my rucksack and stuffed it into my mouth, my mind slid slowly back into panic. There was one question and one question only, rolling around my brain like a ball in a pinball machine, causing me to shudder every time it hit the forefront of my mind. Although it was madness – real madness – I couldn't help but wonder: 'Was she going to eat me?'

Point of No Return

When the doors to the plane were closed and we were taxiing for runway, butterflies began to have twins in my stomach. Or perhaps it was more of a panic attack. It was my first flight alone. I couldn't hear anyone speak English and all the other people on the plane looked decidedly Russian. Dark thoughts began to enter my mind, pooling like drops of water from a leaky tap. Before I left Wales a helpful friend of mine had shown me an article where a Siberian woman roasted her husband on a barbeque and gobbled him up. There were plenty of other horror stories online about British men deceived by Russian honeytraps, left penniless and passport-less after being beaten and robbed. In these stories vulnerable men were usually lured over by hot women who secretly worked for organised gangs or Russian mafia.

4

Being of moderate intelligence I wasn't altogether convinced I would be eaten by Siberian cannibals, but still, I was afraid. It was completely irrational and a bit cowardly, but while I had nobody to talk to and knowing there would be few people who could understand me once we reached our destination, my mind played a few paranoid tricks on me. I even started wondering whether Nastya worked for the KGB and wanted to ensnare me so I could be used to spy on the UK. In hindsight I can see that it was fear of the unknown and nervousness over our impending wedding that caused such silly thoughts, plus I had hardly told anybody the real reason why I was heading to Russia. I didn't know what I would do if Nastya somehow failed to meet me in Moscow. I also didn't know the Russian word for help, or any other Russian for that matter.

Over the four hour flight I managed to turn my fear into excitement and reminded myself that Nastya wasn't likely to eat me or sell me as a sex slave to the mob. During one weekend in Paris, while out walking in broad daylight, we had been stopped in the street by two young people who tried to con me out of my money. It was Nastya who didn't lose her nerve, grabbing me by the arm and forcefully pulling me through the con-artists to the safety of a café. It was Nastya who had seen me safely back to Gare Du Nord station, knowing that my sense of direction was rubbish. I knew that she loved me. I knew from our first meeting in Paris in January 2010.

We had met at the station and hurried back to our hotel where we made love clumsily as two people do when they make love for the first time. Afterwards, while Nastya had a shower, I sat at the edge of the bed and looked out over Paris at night. I was overcome with a sadness that seemed impossible to get past; I was sad that we had so little time together, that we had to part so soon after we had just met, that we lived so far apart from each other and that it would be a struggle to make our relationship work. Nastya seemed to sense this and, without me even noticing that she had left the bathroom, came and held me. In that moment she kept me from falling into myself. It was the most important embrace of my life. I don't know how long she held me for but most of my troubles and internal battles left me there and then. Knowing this, it was crazy to think even for a moment that she could wish me any harm, or look at me like I would taste good with potatoes and tomato sauce.

A Very Long-distance Courtship

I was born Michael Anthony Oliver, or Little Mike, which is what my parents and sisters liked to call me when they wanted to piss me off. This only lasted for the sixteen years it took until I left home and then, after inheriting my mother's genes, I became big Mike; 6ft, slim and with hair that couldn't decide if it belonged on top of a hedgehog or on Clint Eastwood as Dirty Harry. As a conscientious young man I did my homework, left high school, and went on to A-Levels in college, only somewhere along the line something went wrong. I didn't go to university. Instead I found myself working for five years in a high street bank as a mortgage underwriter and general office clerk. It was there that I earned my new name. This is a hotly disputed point between my parents even to this day, but when I was born one of the two decided to give me my father's name, word for word, including middle name. For a minute or so they had discussed calling me Mark, but this was thrown aside as my dad already had an estranged son by this name through a previous marriage.

At twenty, well after I had left home, I toyed with the idea of calling myself Archibald Lasalles, after the long distance runner from the 1981 film *Gallipoli*, starring Mark Lee and Mel Gibson. In school, those who didn't like football were made to run long distance through country lanes to the Greendown pub a few miles away, and back again within the hour. At the same time, in history class, when we were asked to re-enact a scene from history, I chose to be Archie Lasalles on his final run over the front line in World War I, so the name seemed a good one to keep for myself, though it proved a bit mouthy. After two weeks I ditched it.

When I started at the bank in 2002, the boss who was forever kissing my arse for some reason, called me Chairman Mao, as M.A.O. were the initials I signed letters with. It stuck. I didn't hate my birth name, Michael is after all the name of some archangel, and a keyring I bought when I was on a school trip at the age of five had said 'Michael: who is like the lord', but having the same name as my father had left me feeling as though I didn't have an identity of my own and without this I struggled to live as a human being separate from him. However, sat on that plane, my birth name, printed on my ticket was one of the few things I had to identify myself as myself.

My sister Mab, who was born Michelle Anastasia Oliver, had suffered the same identity crisis as me; she was after all another M.A.O. After running through every stage of the education system with flying colours she had gone to live in Japan in 2001, to make a living teaching English while learning the fine art of karaoke.

In March 2006, after years of drudgery, self-loathing, boredom and despair caused by working in a bank, I received a phone call from the pub next to work. It was Mab. I left the office early and told my boss I would have a very long lunch. My sister looked confident; she had brighter eyes and was a shadow of the self-doubting person I had known in previous years. After a few pints she pronounced she was going to be a famous writer and poet, and asked if I would care to be her warm up act. Soon after that I quit my job and started writing full time, taking on a few menial jobs to keep the wolves from the door. Three years later, Mab prepared a show named D-Day and invited me to take part in it, alongside a small army of other poets and writers. As an anti-nationalist she had the idea that we would read to a bilingual

Welsh/English audience on St David's Day while ridiculing nationalism. Many years earlier, while explaining to a friend of a friend my frustration at having failed my Welsh A-level, and how hard it was to integrate with the fluent Welsh-speaking society, she had joked that I may as well have learned Russian; in preparing for the D-Day show I remembered her words and considered them further. I decided to deliver my entire performance in Russian.

Using a series of social networking sites I was able to identify many people who had the words 'Russian translator' as part of their history or interests. After looking at a few candidates and not having the slightest clue who to go for, I thought best to choose one entirely at random. After a brief introduction and some begging, Anastasia Semenova, a telecommunications engineer with a background in literature and translation agreed to translate my poem for free. Not only had I found a translator but I had also found my future wife.

Every day after work I would switch on my computer just to speak to Anastasia (Nastya to her friends) on Facebook Chat. Nastya, being in Krasnoyarsk, Siberia, was seven hours ahead; when it was 5 p.m. for me it was midnight for her. We never had much time to talk but we cherished every minute. At first we found friendship in the fact we had both recently come out of difficult relationships. I had dated a woman from 2006 to 2008, and this union had ended badly. Nastya had lived through a similar relationship, in almost the same time frame. So we confided in each other about how we felt, which felt easier than talking to our other friends because of the very fact that we were two people who hardly knew each other. We were entirely different from one another – perfect opposites – however our friendship strengthened as we were both heartbroken, very lonely, and yet very determined in a pact to steer ourselves away from our past lives and live as independently as we could. This seemed like a fine idea, only the more we talked of independence the more we drew together; and the more we designed our own way in the world the more our desires collided. Although neither of us wanted to be romantically involved with someone else, we couldn't help but forge a romantic bond. Exchanges of personal philosophies led to an exchange of photographs. Exchanges of photos led to exchanges of feelings. At twenty four, Nastya looked very much like a young Sophie Marceau, and although I was four years older, I still had a brilliant head of *Dirty Harry* hair to speak for me. Plus I was a cyclist with a cyclist's frame. Though we had few things in common, besides our ruined love affairs, our fondness for one another grew to the point we couldn't pass a day without a phone call. By Christmas time, we were in love, although I had also become unemployed, couch-surfing the living rooms and kindnesses of friends and relatives.

We had known each other for nearly a year and yet we hadn't actually met face-to-face. In November, to pay for our first meeting I took a part-time job working early hours in a supermarket. Nastya decided that our first encounter would be in Paris in the New Year, on January 7th, which just happened to be Russian Christmas Day. As it was winter and a particularly harsh one at that, the snow and ice had limited the Eurostar travel to only two trains a day. News coverage reported hourly how so many hundreds of people were stranded in St Pancras, London, and it was advised not to travel if you didn't have to. On the morning of the 7th, I left Cardiff for London on the National Express. An hour after we had crossed the Severn Bridge, it was closed due to falling ice. When I arrived at St Pancras, it was heaving, the queue of people went from the ticket office, through ten bendy queue-dividers, right down to the end of the building. I waited for hours and was the last-but-one to board the only train that afternoon.

I arrived in Gare Du Nord at about 8 p.m. Paris time. My French was terrible (still is), and I couldn't find Nastya anywhere.

When I asked a police officer where the main exit was he simply shrugged his shoulders and mumbled something French. Nastya and I phoned each other in desperation, each claiming the other was by the exit of the building, which of course wasn't true; I was by a small, little-used exit for smokers. After much panic Nastya found me and gave me a huge hug, her big brown eyes full of tears. She had arrived in Paris a few hours earlier and had already studied the underground system. She led me to Line 4 where we took the train all the way to Porte d'Orléans, Montrouge, at the end of the line on the South Bank. She had booked us a double bed for the weekend at the hotel Ibis. Needless to say we didn't see much of Paris, although we did venture out once or twice to see the Eiffel tower; because it was winter, and an unusually cold one, there was snow everywhere which made it more romantic. It was as if Nastya had brought Siberia with her.

Paris became our meeting point throughout 2010 as Nastya couldn't enter Britain by any means. In order to obtain even a simple British tourist visa Nastya would have needed to make the equivalent of 30,000 roubles (around £600) a month. At this time she made around 17,500 roubles (£350) a month. I on the other hand was prepared to visit Russia but didn't have the money. It is ironic that while Nastya held a well-respected job as an IT technician, was reasonably well paid where Russia is concerned, was qualified as a translator and engineer and was a trained pianist, her movements were restricted by global politics and the economics of the day. Whereas I, a poorly-trained unofficial nobody and self-appointed poet, could travel anywhere, provided I had some dosh. Even a full-time, minimum-wage job would have afforded me enough money to visit Russia. However, in 2010, the hotel Ibis in Montrouge, Paris, was our second home on occasional weekends. By our next romantic getaway in Paris we even had our own favourite restaurant, which although we don't remember its name *can* be found by taking the underground to Boulevard St Michel and walking two streets in from the river in the direction of the Eiffel tower. At the point you are completely lost, the restaurant is on the left.

It was early on in our affair that we decided to marry. Our long-distance courtship was taking its toll on us; I guess all people in these kinds of situations find it hard. Not only that but I couldn't really say I had a home to go to and because of the global economic crash there was little chance of me finding a regular, decent job in the UK. British immigration law states that I would need full-time employment and a permanent residence in order for Nastya to be allowed to live in the UK. Pigs might fly by the time that happened and so the only option available to us was for me to move to Russia.

It turns out that finding someone who wants to marry you isn't the hardest part of getting married. For a British citizen to marry abroad one needs a lot of forms. Firstly you must apply for a Certificate of No Impediment to Marry (CNIM). Once you have this it needs an Apostille (this is a stamp from the Foreign Office based in Milton Keynes). A standard Russian tourist visa at the time had to be applied for forty-five days before the intended travel date which prevented me from booking really cheap flights. Once I applied, I had to wait around two weeks for a decision. This was to allow the FSB (Federal Security Service formally known as the KGB) adequate time to investigate me (the application was very long and asked if I had any 'special skills' or military training).

When I had my passport back, I thought I was in the clear. Research on several Russian travel websites soon informed me that when I arrived in Moscow I would still need to get everything translated and stamped again. Then all my documents, both original and translated, would need to be presented to an International Wedding Court. Worse than this I read that we could only be married a month or two months after application, which would have been impossible with a single month's visa;

although the same websites stated that the wedding courts would likely accept bribes to make it sooner. Determined that we wouldn't be separated by bureaucracy, or economics, I left for Moscow with a suitcase full of warm clothes, and a rucksack loaded with Jaffa Cakes.

Trans-Siberian. March 31ˢᵗ 2011. Moscow — Krasnoyarsk

The doors to all the wagons of the train opened simultaneously, and a number of heavyset, extremely intimidating female guards stepped out in black greatcoats and grey ushankas (classic Russian trapper's hat). Our passports and papers were checked and we boarded. The engine itself wasn't anything like I had expected. I had been hoping for some great big steam engine, instead it was a large industrial one. Like a green brick on wheels.

There are three different classes of tickets on the Trans-Siberian. The first and most expensive is a compartment all of your own. The second is a compartment of four bunks – two lower bunks that convert into beds, and two upper bunks which are always beds – and third class, which I am told is six bunks to a compartment. We had chosen second class. I wasn't actually aware of the etiquette and so as soon as we entered our compartment I sat on the seat opposite Nastya. This seemed only natural, but not long after I had sat down, a large, muscular Russian man entered and gave me The Look. I was sat in his seat, which would also double as his bed, so I changed sides quickly.

Sat next to Nastya, with our knees pressed against the tiny table in the centre, it was hard to imagine how anyone could travel third class. But people do, and often. In Russia, because of its size, it's normal for people to commute to meetings via two, three, four or sometimes eight-day journeys. Our compartment, second class, felt like a sardine tin and for the next three days that sardine tin was home. There was a dining cabin on board the train, although eating there would have required leaving our bags with a complete stranger. Having anticipated this situation, we had bought a picnic – some sausage meat, a large pack of cheese, some Brie, a loaf of bread, a pack of pastrami and a few sachets of herbal tea – from a half decent supermarket we had found earlier that morning, which surprisingly sold a wide selection of Western produce.

When it was time to prepare our meals, which involved cutting our bread and cheese on the *itsy witsy* table, our travelling companion, although large and scary, turned out to be the perfect gentleman and would always leave for a walk up and down the train. I regret not learning his name or plucking up the courage to thank him for his good manners and generosity before he left the train for good. The Trans-Siberian is a popular tourist attraction and so it was normal to find a Brit on the train with an extremely poor grasp of the Russian language. Therefore our companion only communicated through Nastya, and only to make polite conversation or to ask if we would like to share his beer. The afternoon was long – from the small window we could only see pines and birches morning and night – except for a few stations, which all looked alike. There was no shower facility and the toilet made a high-pitched sound when flushed that hurt our ears if we weren't quick enough to cover them. Anyone who takes that train across the whole of Russia is not only going to have severe cramp by the end of their trip, but is likely to smell as bad as a wet dog that has been rolling in his own poop.

Despite all this, our first day passed without incident. However, as we hadn't got to know our travelling companion yet, after he procured a 6-inch Bowie knife from his boot to cut his meat in the afternoon, I found it near impossible to sleep that first night. Nastya had brought her own knife to cut meat but it was only an inch long. I knew this would have been of little use in defence against a burly Russian who carried a blade big enough to chop off my head in one fell swoop. Lying there on my bunk above

Nastya's as we were hurtling further into Russia in the dead of night I was struck by fear and panic. With the ceiling of the wagon so close to my head I occasionally reached up, put my palms against it and pressed myself deeper into my bunk, as if this would somehow make me safer. As the hours went by I began to doze slightly, my mind filled with images of Moscow.

As the plane touched down in Sheremetyevo airport, I could see it was going to be hard to dispel the stereotypical view of Russia I had come to know from Hollywood films. A bleak sky mirrored the dirty snow surrounding the airport; the blanket of grey-white absorbing the airport sign's blood-red glow without a trace of reflection. I was met at Sheremetyevo by Nastya, who had taken the Trans-Siberian to Moscow three days earlier and had arrived that morning. She had already booked us a double bed in a hostel where we planned to stay for two nights. I had arranged to meet an up-and-coming Russian poet in Red Square the following day and we also needed to get documents translated. To give you an idea of the scale of Moscow, it took nearly four hours to travel from the airport to the other side of the city (it takes four hours to travel from Cardiff to Heathrow Airport, via National Express). Moscow could be a country all of its own. It is a vast maze of roads and underground train stations. I had left the UK on a four hour flight at around 1.15 p.m. GMT and arrived in Moscow at about 8.30 p.m. because of the time difference. After travelling across the capital and checking into our hostel it was close to midnight, so there was little time for anything other than sleep.

My first day in Moscow had begun with a trip through the underground to a translation office in order to have my CNIM, Apostille and passport translated. We left photocopies of my documents there and went for my first lunch in a Russian café. The food was worse than anything I could have imagined. The jacket potato I ordered was not potato, but Smash, smothered onto a rubbery potato skin. The sausage was not actual meat, but rather some kind of Spam-like meat substitute. The bacon wasn't actual bacon but a rolled-out Spam-substitute with bacon colouring. I discovered that all the crap you wouldn't even feed to a stray dog is sold to humans in Russia; not only that, but many of the products available are also out of date. Even the packets of cigarettes I bought should have been binned months earlier. I assumed this was due to the global economic crash of 2007 but Nastya assured me that the decline in quality of products had begun in the late nineties.

After our delicious Smash potato meal, Nastya lead me through the underground once more to meet the poet Nikitin on Red Square. Evgeny Nikitin is another person I had met online while I was looking to make good connections with Russian poets. He was one of the founding members of the Moscow Poetry Club as well as being the newly-appointed editor for the very famous Soviet and Russian poet Yevgeny Yevtushenko. Earlier that day, Nastya and I had visited Red Square so that I could take a few photographs. As we stood around admiring the scenery, we had heard screams. When we turned to see what the commotion was we saw people running. From between two buildings what looked like a white wall of ice – or huge cloud of white dust from a Hollywood movie – came pouring out over the Muscovites. It had taken only a few seconds to reach us. The wall was, in fact, a sudden blizzard made of heavy chunks of snow and hail. We fled like everyone else and took shelter in one of the subways.

As soon as Nikitin had joined us, we headed straight for a coffee bar of Nikitin's choosing, in case another storm hit us. Over English tea with milk he told me the story of his first collection of poetry. It was sold in a shop for contemporary books not far from where we were. In previous months, the militia had requested that this shop be closed down because some of the content of the books they stocked were deemed subversive and because it was also a meeting place for modern poets and political thinkers. The shop wasn't shut down due to some legal technicality; however a week later it was mysteriously set alight by persons unknown, and all published copies of Nikitin's collection perished. The shop had since been refurbished and so Nikitin offered to take us there. I wish I could remember the address but it's probably for the best that I cannot. The shop itself was off a main road, down an alleyway, through a side door, up three flights of stairs, along a corridor and on the other side of a large steel door. When we arrived Nikitin couldn't show me any of the books he had wished to, as there was a meeting of political thinkers and poets who were clearly in the middle of an important debate. We listened for five minutes before deciding that it wasn't safe to stay there. Had the militia stormed the building, had they asked for my papers and seen I was British visiting on a tourist visa, I could have been arrested, interrogated and/or deported. Instead Nikitin led Nastya and me back to the main street where we parted company and walked in opposite directions. It was already early evening and the cold was beginning to bite. Before going back to our hostel, Nastya and I went to a mini supermarket to get a few things necessary for a light supper. We were both surprised to find the shop almost completely empty, except for a few cans of a red fizzy drink made in the Caucasus and a few large bottles of water. We left with two bottles of the fizzy red stuff only to be disappointed later.

When we arrived back at our hostel at around 10 p.m. I noticed that there were many militia on our street, an unusually large number of them, and they seemed to be coming from a building across from ours. Nastya informed me that we were actually sleeping across from their headquarters. Militia (pronounced mee-leet-see-ya) are everywhere; they are partly police, partly immigration authority and partly intelligence service. They are the first thing you notice when you step off the plane and they remain omnipresent for the rest of your trip. I had learned from the Russian visa company I used that they have the power to stop and search anyone. It is said that if they find you without your passport and papers to hand, and you do not have sufficient money to bribe them, you can be deported. They are to be avoided at all times. I did not sleep so easy that night knowing there was an army of them across the street.

We left early the following morning, carrying my luggage which weighed around eleven kilos. When travelling in any foreign country I think it's always best to travel light in order to avoid any unnecessary delays, plus it's easier to run away if you get into trouble. After picking up our newly-translated documents in the centre of Moscow and purchasing two tickets for the Trans-Siberian we made our way to Yaroslavsky train station, north east of the city centre. This was actually the most frightening part of my journey. Yaroslavsky station was teaming with all kinds of unsavoury people. They swarm around you under the pretence of wanting to sell you something while they take mental notes of where your money is most likely hidden. Not only that but there were around two hundred militia, standing around like demigods, laughing among themselves, automatic rifles loosely slung over their shoulders like harmless rucksacks; some swinging their weapons around like a child would swing a toy. Never have I heard that little voice inside of me shouting so loud 'Get out of here! Get out of here now!' We couldn't get out of there right away though. We were to wait on the platform while the train had its interior cleaned. I needed a cigarette. I took out my tobacco and papers to make a roll up and was quickly scorned by Nastya, who chose that moment to inform me that nobody in Russia smoked roll ups; people would think I was smoking drugs and would likely inform the militia. I looked around. A few people were watching so I finished my smoke as casually as I could and hoped for the best.

We hadn't had to walk through any barriers to get to our platform. Absolutely anyone could come and stand next to the train. Among obvious passengers there were several babushkas (old women) without luggage, just brown parcels in their hands. They approached everyone on the platform and, one by one, begged us to take their parcels for them. Nastya refused bluntly in a very harsh tone. I knew why, of course. Although they seemed to be normal old ladies, who were trying to get a stranger to do them the kindness of delivering a parcel for them because they hadn't the money for postage, there could have been anything in those packages. With Nastya's best Siberian 'Go away or I will get nasty' tone and a wave of the hand, they left us to bother someone else. This reminded me of a story Nigel, a friend of mine from Cardiff, had told me weeks before I departed. A Russian friend of his who wanted to attend some sort of conference in Bulgaria was only allowed an exit visa if he would agree to deliver a package for the KGB. However that incident was during the Soviet years, and as I wasn't actually bargaining for anything myself, I'm confident those Yaroslavsky babushkas weren't working for the secret service. They had a look of desperation on their faces and were dressed in worn-out winter coats, rubber shoes that looked decades old, and head scarves that didn't appear anywhere near capable of keeping the cold out. Some had even been close to crying.

By the afternoon of our second day on the train I was too tired to be afraid anymore. I had forgotten to bring a toothbrush and so Nastya asked the wagon guard to bring me a travelling kit. This consisted of a tiny toothbrush, a small sachet of toothpaste, a bar of soap, a tiny folded towel in a sachet, and a pair of paper slippers. On the Trans-Siberian, like anywhere in Russia, it is considered rude and unhygienic not to wear slippers, even if you're the kind of person who walks in your socks. Regardless of not being a slipper person I was glad of the comforts that were included in the kit and wore my paper slippers every day.

It should also be noted that while on this extremely exciting and frightening train journey I carried two mobile phones. One, an expensive all-singing all-dancing touch screen thing which had more functions than I can count; and the other, a five pound supermarket mobile, which made calls and sent texts. While travelling through four time zones from Moscow to Krasnoyarsk, my flashy phone went all flashy. It told the wrong time constantly, changed the time as and when it fancied, and in general seemed in a state of panic. However, my cheap mobile updated the time when we broke through into a new time zone, welcomed me to my new destination via text, informed me of the new tariffs and offered numbers for emergencies relevant to that area. This is the phone I still use today. It doesn't sing or dance, or allow me to check emails, or locate my GPS position, but it doesn't panic; and while you are travelling through Russia and are likely to panic, you need a phone that will remain calm.

Every few hundred miles, the train needed to stop, either at a station to pick up and drop off passengers, or at a docking area to refuel, take on water and fresh supplies of food. These stops are crucial for leg stretching and getting some fresh air because the windows in the sleeping compartments don't open. Even though the large female wagon guards would dress down while the train was in motion, each time it stopped they would always stand tall, just to the side of the wagon entrance, wearing great coats and ushankas, looking official.

At these stops, some of which seemed miles from anywhere, there were often babushkas that looked no different from those I had seen in the train station, waiting with goods that they hung on strings under their shabby winter coats. I didn't buy anything from them but was glad and sad each time I saw them. I admired their tenacity and will to keep on going, but was sad that they had to endure what appeared to be a very tough way to make a living. When I awoke on the morning of day three, our travelling companion had vanished. Instead there was a different Russian man on the top bunk opposite mine. This one was much uglier than the first and didn't seem to care much for our company. Thankfully he got off in the late afternoon in Novosibirsk and wasn't replaced by anybody. Our next station and final destination was a little less than twelve hours away, and so Nastya and I got to spend the rest of Day Three alone. As I was feeling slightly sick and undernourished we ordered some soup and a plate of chips from the dining cabin, only too happy to take our order and deliver it. When the tiny portions of food were delivered it became clear why they were so happy. It appeared that food from the dining cabin wasn't any different from café food, in that it was undercooked, and the portions were only fit to keep a starving rat alive a few more hours. However, I was glad for the soup, although it tasted like boiled mayonnaise. Nastya told me this was a throwback from the early 1990s when people added mayo or sour cream to their food to make it seem more than it was.

It was after my hearty and delicious meal that Nastya and I got to live the James Bond/Natasha Romanova experience, and have sex on a train (see Ian Fleming's *From Russia with Love*). I can't be too explicit about this as I wish to avoid embarrassing my wife, but what I can say is that sex on a train is great and must be considered by all horny tourists who take the Trans-Siberian. Undressing a gorgeous young Russian woman, while travelling at high speed through the wilderness of Siberia is a huge turn on, and knowing the wagon guard lady might enter at any moment to empty the bin or hoover the floor just heightens the adrenalin level that little bit more. It has to be said that by the end of Day Three, I didn't care where we were going, which country we were in, or how many big scary Russians were near. This was good because the following day I had to meet my parents-in-law to be, both likely to be big scary Russians.

On the morning of Day Four the train began to slow at 5 or 6 a.m. Krasnoyarsk time and we were woken by the radio. Each cabin had a speaker in the corner by the window, which until then was used only to announce stations, and how long we would be stopped. On that morning they were playing a long romantic song, sung in English, called 'My Krasnoyarsk', which was both lovely and appropriate because we were about to stop at Krasnoyarsk. We brushed our teeth quickly, gathered and packed our things into my bags and watched out of the window as the train slowly ground to a halt. The view was unlike any other so far. Krasnoyarsk was a large city surrounded by dachas (wooden houses) and, to the south and west, these were shadowed by snowcapped mountains. For Nastya this view was commonplace since she had lived in Krasnoyarsk all her life, but for me it was breathtaking. As I stepped off the train I saw a large black steam engine parked on a concrete platform – a memorial perhaps for the time when the Trans-Siberian had been more romantic.

Transaero Flight UN158. April 26th 2011. Krasnoyarsk — Moscow

Though it cost all the money that had been gifted to us after our wedding, Nastya came with me to Moscow on the Easter Monday. This was unnecessarily extravagant, but she had insisted, and as we had no plans for a honeymoon it seemed like a good idea to be tourists for a day in Moscow. She didn't want to be without me for a minute longer than she had to. I was glad anyway, because although Yemelyanovo Airport near Krasnoyarsk was apparently international, none of the announcements were given in English. Even Nastya had seemed confused over which plane was ours because there had been two flights leaving for Moscow at the exact same time, going to completely different airports. I knew that if I had been there alone chances are I would have ended up on the wrong flight.

Sat by the window, I watched as we charged down the runway into the early morning sky. Siberia felt so alien to me – all those trees, mountains and little wooden houses. It was hard to picture myself living there, though I had been a guest for a full month already. I didn't know what the future would hold but I knew I would have to return. We had no other choice. There was so much to do and so many decisions to make. I wasn't sure if I could make the transition to Siberian life.

Oblivious to my internal struggles, Nastya smiled. She was excited that we were travelling together, or she seemed to be anyway. Before leaving the apartment there had been a moment where she began crying, but she quickly stifled her tears for my benefit. I had done the same the evening before, lying awake on the bed while Nastya slept. My mind simply wouldn't switch off. As tired as I was, sitting next to Nastya, who was now my wife, it seemed a shame to sleep. I wanted to remember every minute of our last day together. We said nothing to each other the whole time, but swapped occasional knowing glances. When she finally fell asleep, as I knew she would, I thought back over my time in Krasnoyarsk.

Pushkin Square

Stepping off the train onto land felt much like stepping off a ship. My body was undulating from three days and nights of rolling over tracks. It was hard to stand up straight without rocking back and fore. This sensation lasted for a few days. Poor Nastya had it worse as she had come to Moscow by train and returned the same way. We were met at the station by Nastya's Aunt Olga who drove us to Nastya's city apartment where she lived with her parents. Driving or being driven in Russia is a totally different experience from driving in the West. The roads are full of potholes, and when I say potholes, I'm talking the kind of pots you grow trees in. All the cars swerve and weave around both sides of the road to avoid falling into them. Not only that but they drive at speed. Russians remember the location of each pothole like Westerners remember the location of speed cameras and tight corners. When we arrived at the apartment I was closer to a state of panic again.

City apartments and residential areas in Russia look more like Beirut that anywhere else. The buildings are tall and rectangular and are constructed from large concrete block or really big red bricks. The block work, while mostly straight enough to keep a building up, was obviously constructed haphazardly. It is not unusual to see a brick wall, which should be the flat face of a building, full of small twists and turns. Build a wall out of empty boxes with your eyes closed, and you're not too far away from pre-1991 Russian construction. The main courtyards of these buildings are mostly large concrete slabs that also appear to overlap and have big spaces in between for you to fall into. Everything seems thrown together.

To enter the building we had to pass through a large armoured door, plated with thick steel panels that could only be opened with a magnetic key or the combination to the keypad on the side. Once inside we walked up four flights of the most badly-laid concrete steps in the whole world to reach Nastya's steel front door. I stepped inside the narrow hallway, made narrower by a huge brown wardrobe on the left, and removed my shoes, which immediately let out foot-smell. I was worried for a second that Nastya's parents' first impression of me would be pongy feet; I didn't have time to worry. With Nastya and Olga behind me, jostling for space to take off their shoes and coats, I was quickly pushed into the middle of the hallway. The whole place seemed yellowish, like white walls after someone has smoked for a hundred years; and there was a strong whiff of feet other than my own. As I kicked my shoes gently to the side of the hall I saw huge piles of boots that had been shoved haphazardly into the bottom of the wardrobe as both a quick tidy up and a way to mask their scent.

Raising my gaze from the floor I was faced with two shadowy figures, Nastya's parents. I had no idea what to say. I couldn't even force out a hello. Our eyes were locked together. Their inquisitive glare troubled me before their eyes began to smile. We were greeted in Russian and herded into the small kitchen at the end of the hall, where Nastya's mum, Nataliya Petrovna, had prepared some deer meat and herbal tea.

Although the short version of her mother's name was Natasha, I had been cautioned by Nastya to always refer to her as Nataliya Petrovna, as a sign of respect. Everyone spoke in Russian, which of course I didn't understand, though thankfully this didn't last for too long. Nastya's parents simply wanted to have a good look at me. Which they did – a good long look. Though the kitchen table was slightly bigger than the one on the train we were all struggling for space – the kitchen itself was not much bigger than our train compartment had been. We were hungry; very hungry. Nastya had asked her mother to cook something for when we arrived, and I had visions of a large meal, with sauces and various vegetables. I don't know why I imagined it would be like that. Wishful thinking probably. I was so hungry I thought I could have eaten anything, but that wasn't true. When two half-cooked meatballs of nondescript meat were placed before me, I could have cried. I cut one in half and put some in my mouth, as did Nastya. They were cold on the inside. Out of politeness I kept eating, washing down each mouthful with tea. When I had managed to make the first one disappear Nastya told me that her mother confessed to rushing the food and we didn't have to finish if we didn't want to. I left the other ball on the plate. After giving me one final look over, the parents left, taking Olga with them, and we were free to sleep off our travel weariness.

I spent the following morning familiarising myself with the apartment. Normally it would have been inhabited by Nataliya Petrovna's eighty-seven-year-old mother, Baba Ira, but she was in hospital following an infection caused by an ingrowing toenail. Nastya's parents had gone to stay at their dacha on the west of the city to allow Nastya and myself the freedom to walk around the apartment half-dressed, which we did most of the time because it was impossible to turn down the heating. As that day was Sunday, and there was nowhere Nastya could really think of taking me that would be open, we organised our papers ready to take to the wedding court the next day.

Before going to the wedding office on the Monday morning we had to obtain my registration paper. This is a separate document from the immigration card that was given to me at the airport. Your registration paper must be applied for at a post office or local immigration office (UFMS) in whatever city you visit, and must be obtained within seven days of arrival in any city that you plan to stay at for more than a week. Leaving the apartment to walk to the post office I felt acutely aware of how vulnerable I was being a pre-registered Westerner. Even though I still had six days left to obtain this document I knew that if I was stopped by the militia on our short journey there was a risk I could be asked to hand over all the money I had.

From the outside it was impossible to tell the building housed an office at all, as many shops in suburban areas and offices in Russia all look very much alike. The queue inside the post office was horrendous: rows of babushkas waiting to pick up their pension money. When it was our turn, we were informed that they would need a photocopy of my passport, immigration card and Nastya's residential permit. We copied these at a building not far away. Back in the post office Nastya had to fill in two copies of the same form, which were are as long and complex as my visa application, except the boxes to write in were tiny and only perfectly handwritten block capitals were accepted. Many mistakes and many forms later, we finally had it right and so queued one more time to hand everything in and pay the few hundred rouble fee (equivalent of a few pounds). I was now a completely legal resident of Krasnoyarsk city for a month. Should the militia try to squeeze money out of me, I now had the power to threaten them with a harassment investigation by the British Embassy. Still, I felt uneasy whenever I walked past them or if they drove past us. This was their country and they had the ability to arrest me, deport me or make me disappear entirely if they felt like it; having an embassy two thousand miles away in Moscow wasn't actually much of a comfort.

Opposite the post office we caught the 91 bus, which took half an hour to reach the city centre. Bus journeys in Krasnoyarsk are not a pleasant experience. Most vehicles are old second-hand machines from Germany, Korea or China, and still have emergency exit signs in the language of their native country. The interiors are spent from about fifty years of use and there are never enough seats. There are no ticket machines either. Instead, a painfully thin girl or large middle-aged woman walks up and down the bus collecting thirteen roubles off every new passenger. As the bus moves at speed and weaves all over the road to avoid potholes, it's appreciated if you have the correct change ready, which I didn't. Nastya paid the twenty-six roubles and the collection girl tore two tickets off the reel in her hand and passed them to me, while giving me a very sour look. In Russia it is still frowned upon to let your woman pay on the buses or at restaurants. In a land where women are raised to cook while the men are raised to either hunt or go to work, equality is a word very little used.

Stood on the practically seat-less bus to Pushkin Square, I noticed how nearly every vehicle except for the buses had blacked out windows, some even with blacked-out windscreens. It seemed as though people did whatever they could to remain unseen. I later learned that it was illegal to have the front windows of a car darkened and that the militia did stop vehicles regularly forcing the drivers to scrape off the darkening plastic cover there and then.

The wedding court was yet another building that could have been anything. The reception was unmanned so we had to go through to the back office to register, which was really simple. As fortune would have it, not only was getting married really cheap, but they had a space on the Friday of that week; no bribery was needed. We booked our wedding for 10.30 a.m. on Friday the 8th April. It was just four days away and we felt relieved. The rest of the week was filled with shopping. We needed two things – wedding rings and new boots. The rings were an easy affair as Nastya much preferred silver to gold. The rings Nastya chose were basic and cost the equivalent of £12 each. The boots were a much more complex affair. Russians are crazy about boots and like to have a new pair for all special occasions. We went to a large complex that sold only boots; millions of them, boots in every shape and size. I don't remember how long we spent there but I do remember being a bit short-tempered after the fiftieth pair tried were still no good. Nastya finally decided on a pair from a high street store towards the end of the day, more through desperation than for love of the actual boots. I bought a pair of black shoes in the morning, from the first men's shoe shop we entered, and took all of ten minutes to choose them, which is a pretty long time for me.

On the evening before our wedding, Nataliya Petrovna came over to the apartment to wish us well and to interrogate me. Neither of Nastya's parents knew me very well and they needed to make sure their daughter was making the right decision. It must have seemed odd to them that someone from an affluent country would travel all that way to marry a Siberian girl. British men also have a reputation in Russia for treating women badly and spending their wives' money. Russian men are gentlemen in comparison; they do things like holding doors open and take off a woman's coat for her when she gets home. I told her that although there had been a few short periods where I had little or no work, I had a pretty sound work-ethic, and though I had never taken off a woman's coat, it wouldn't be a hardship. She seemed satisfied with that but still asked 'Are there no women in Wales?' to which I replied 'Yes, dozens of them.' Her final question was 'Scientists have said that a person's life partner is usually born within a few miles of them; what do you think of this?' My answer was 'Scientists also once said that the world was flat.' The discussion was over. NO THEY DID NOT.

The one thing we had overlooked and almost completely forgotten was our need to find an official translator for our nuptials; the law stated that we must have one as my Russian was appalling, and still is. On the evening before our wedding we emailed everyone in the vicinity who could speak both languages and might be free. It was a tall order as most translators work Monday to Friday. Our savior came in the shape of Kostya, a Russian missionary who had travelled the world doing good deeds. He didn't even want paying, although we bought him a box of chocolates for his kindly efforts.

The morning of the wedding felt like any other morning. We wore jeans, shirts, new boots, and normal winter coats, and I took a black ushanka just in case it snowed. We caught a taxi as we were worried all the buses might have magically disappeared, and so we arrived in plenty of time. Kostya came by foot and arrived five minutes after us. The wedding ceremony was very simple. We sat in plastic chairs opposite a wooden desk in the same back office where we had registered two days before. A woman in smart casual dress read through the laws and official stuff of marriage; Kostya translated; we said 'I do' and it was done. Nastya shed a few tears while I tried to contain my nervous laughter. The certificate, which seemed to have been printed before we arrived, was handed to me, as I was now the 'head of the family'. We were wished good luck and farewell and left the office no more than fifteen minutes after we had entered.

Although, legally, we had to use the international wedding court, we could have had another much larger church ceremony afterwards. Most weddings in Krasnoyarsk are lavish affairs, with showy receptions, that finish with a limousine sightseeing tour of the city. Siberian newlyweds simply love posing for the camera and like to have their picture taken near the Yenisei as well as some of the older, Orthodox church buildings. By contrast our wedding had been very modest, to the point that we neglected to take any pictures at all. I had worried that our small ceremony might not have been enough for Nastya, but each time we spoke about it she affirmed that she didn't care to waste lots of money on one single day, when we had a whole future together to look forward to.

To celebrate our marriage, Nastya and I had decided that we would locate one of the very few Irish bars in Krasnoyarsk and have a pint of Guinness. What better way is there to celebrate? It took us a few hours to find one and once we did we discovered that it wouldn't be open until 1 p.m., which left us an hour to kill. Nastya knew of a café conveniently close so we went there for a betrothal breakfast while we waited; this was a mistake. The café, albeit modern, sold the usual type of mush found in most Russian cafés. We ordered mashed potato that was poured out of a machine like a drinks dispenser, and two portions of some kind of meat type thing which was as bland as roasted cardboard. The Irish bar wasn't much better. Yes it *was* decked out in green garb with Irish pictures on the walls, but there wasn't an Irishman in sight; we had to put our coats in the cloakroom (at the time I assumed this was in case we carried weapons, but later I learned it's standard across Russia), and not only was the pint poured to the little white marker line below the top of the glass, but each pint was a fiver. Still, I will never forget that drink. It was real Guinness, and we were newlyweds enjoying a pint of the good stuff, early on a Friday afternoon, in an Eastern Siberia that was still covered in snow. That one pint really hit the spot, so we collected our coats and went home, where we fell onto the bed and slept for the rest of the afternoon. I woke in the early evening to find Nastya, Nataliya Petrovna, Dima (my new brother-in-law), and several other distant relations preparing food in the kitchen and living room. Now we were going to celebrate Russian-style. In our wedding preparations Nastya and I had completely missed the need to throw a party, let alone invite family over, because we had been consumed with obtaining the right paperwork and getting me to Siberia.

The impromptu wedding banquet consisted of deer meat, hunted and killed by my now father-in-law Boris, and cooked in a variety of different ways by my now mother-in-law Nataliya Petrovna; and contrary to what we think of the Russians in the West it wasn't a boozy affair. Collectively we enjoyed two or three bottles of champagne before we called it a night. Nastya and I were left to put the dishes away and mop up the remnants of the large honey cake someone had bought instead of a wedding cake. There are a few customs in Russia when it comes to marriage, one being a large wedding pie that only the newlyweds can eat, and the one who devours the most is supposed to be the boss of the marriage from there on in. We didn't observe this or any other custom. It's not that we didn't want a wedding pie, because I especially wanted one, it was simply that in the rush to get married, with all the worry about documents, stamps and registration papers, we forgot to think about any of the things we would have enjoyed after the wedding, like giant pies and parties.

Dissolution of the Soviet Union

Before deciding on my voyage to Krasnoyarsk, Nastya and I had discussed getting married in Copenhagen, because we wouldn't have had to jump through hoops to obtain visas, and a company there offered an attractive wedding package for couples who lived in separate countries. At the last minute Nastya changed her mind, thinking it would be better for us to marry in her city so I could also get to know it a little, which would help us decide where we would spend our future. I had never heard of the city before. My knowledge of Russian geography was limited, as in I couldn't have told you where Moscow was if my life depended on it. It was only after I landed that Nastya informed me that I was bang, smack in the middle of Siberia. When we had courted online and in Paris, all of our talk was about being together, being apart, and missing each other. Later we spoke of legal matters:

visas and certificates. In all that time, I hadn't actually given a thought to asking where Krasnoyarsk was, or even looking it up on the map; and consequently found myself in the most central part of Russia not really knowing where I was in the world. Which may sound a bit foolish, but after Nastya and I fell in love, I would have taken a flight anywhere as long as she was waiting for me there. There had been too many failed romantic affairs in my mid-twenties, where I hadn't the guts to take a leap of faith. I'm not sure why that was, but I do know that with Nastya it felt easier to let go of who I was, or had been, and forget my possessions and my limited view of the world. Meeting Natsya had enabled me to break free of the internal restraints that had broken hearts, including my own, in the past.

With the three weeks I had left on my visa, I was free to explore the city, learning all that I should have *before* I went there. For example, I never knew that Russia is divided into eighty-three different parts: two dozen republics, krais, oblasts, and autonomous okrugs. Though I can't tell you what the difference is between a krai and an oblast. I'm not quite sure anyone can. Krasnoyarsk Krai is the biggest of the krais and covers about 13% of Russia's total territory. It's hard to really take in its size, though as a rough guide it is about one hundred times bigger than Wales, and slightly smaller than the moon.

Krasnoyarsk Krai is divided again into forty-four different districts, many of which have long, unpronounceable names like Nizhneingashsky and Zaozyorny. Krasnoyarsk city is the administrative centre of Krasnoyarsk Krai and is itself divided into seven further districts: Kirovsky, Leninsky, Oktyabrsky, Sovetsky, Sverdlovsky, Tsentralny, and Zheleznodorozhny. We lived in Oktyabrsky. It's a bit like one of those Russian matryoshka dolls that decrease in size when you pull their heads off, the seven city districts being at the centre. Oktyabrsky sits inside Krasnoyarsk city which sits in Krasnoyarsk Krai which sits in Siberia which sits in Russia. Russia is the really big doll, being over eight hundred times the size of Wales.

Krasnoyarsk city is the third largest city in Siberia, after Novosibirsk and Omsk. While Cardiff is about 140 km² with a population of around 350,000 people, Krasnoyarsk city is a little over twice the size but with three times the population. It's such a big place that you would think that I would have heard of it before. That's one of the things I find most annoying about my education and about the UK. I know at least a dozen people who can name all the states of America the USA and know most of the cities. Britain has become so Americanised Yanki(fied) that it is taken as read that when someone says a place name in America USA you automatically know where they're talking about. Nobody ever asked if I knew the great little café on the corner of Ulitsa Surikova and Prospekt Mira.

Krasnoyarsk is actually famous in some parts of the world for several different reasons:

1. It is built around a junction of the Trans-Siberian Railway;
2. It is one of Russia's largest producers of aluminium;
3. It was a major centre of the Gulag system;
4. It houses the fifth largest hydroelectric station in the world;
5. In 1749, a 700 kg meteorite was found 145 miles south of the city and it was the first of its kind. Made from an unknown and as yet unclassified type of iron, it was registered as a pallasite, as the scientist examining it was named Peter Pallas, even though the actual discovery was made by a man named Medvedev.
6. In the late 1970s, Abalakovo, a city near Krasnoyarsk, housed a phased array radar station, which frightened Americans the USA because it violated the Anti-Ballistic Missile Treaty. The treaty stated that the radars had to be on the periphery of national territory and had to face outwards; the radar near Krasnoyarsk

was in the middle of the country and faced Siberia. After heavy negotiations in September 1989, the facility was eventually dismantled. It was all a waste of time, however, as in 2001 George W. Bush gave Russia notice of the United States' intention of withdrawal from the treaty and withdrew six months later. It was the first time in recent history that ~~America~~ USA had withdrawn from a major international arms treaty and was a huge blow to the Nuclear Non-Proliferation Treaty, which is now almost completely ignored.

There are several other features of Krasnoyarsk that make the city unique from any other in Russia. One of those is the Stolby nature reserve, a 17,000-hectare area of outstanding natural beauty south of the Yenisei River. It is filled with giant pillars of volcanic rock that were forged millions of years ago when the Sayan mountains, the range between north-western Mongolia and southern Siberia, were pushed up out of the ground by pulses of magma from the Earth's core. Stolby which is otherwise known as 'the land of forest giants' takes its name from the Russian word 'stolb', which translates as 'pillar'. It is hugely popular with rock climbers who flock from all over the world to test themselves against the pillars. It is also a hotspot for scientists who come to study the wildlife. Stolby is a reserve for thousands of rare species of plants as well as birds, wild cats and insects. It is a little too wild for my liking as when there is a lack of berries and nuts in the taiga hungry bears have been known to stroll into Stolby looking for people's leftovers or unattended children.

There are an estimated 200,000 brown bears in the world, and it just so happens that half of them live in Russia. Worse than this, Siberian bears are said to be larger than your average grizzly and unfortunately human flesh *is* on their menu. During my first month in Krasnoyarsk there were seven reported bear attacks. These happened around populated areas on the outskirts of the city where people live in their dachas during the summer period. Bears, it seems, will spy someone lying with their eyes closed, then venture in for a munch. In one case, a local resident out gathering mushrooms came across a bear with cubs. The beast attacked the man and ripped off his scalp. Luckily, a local forester found him, and took him to hospital. Other than complete shock and a lack of scalp, the man came away relatively unhurt.

Besides bears, there is a long list of other ferocious man-eating beasties like wild cats and wolves. Although the chances of running into a tiger in the forests are remote, as they are nearly extinct in the wild, the possibility of running into a pack of wolves isn't. In early 2011, a super pack of wolves, numbering four hundred was reported to have killed thirty horses in just four days in the Northern town of Verkhoyansk, due to a lack of wild rabbits. Besides tigers, the smaller more agile Siberian lynx also lives in the surrounding forests, and although smaller than the native tigers, the lynx of Siberia are the largest found anywhere, and can grow to twice the size of their North American relation. The worst creature however, and the most feared, is the Siberian grass tick. This little critter is no bigger than a head louse, but can be much more harmful. From a blade of grass, this tick can jump onto your skin. Once on your body it eats its way into your flesh where it secretes a poison which causes a disease known as the Siberian tick-borne encephalitis virus; this virus attacks the central nervous system. There are a long list of nasty symptoms, the worst being paralysis, and death. Nastya says that if you are bitten and poisoned, then you have to go to hospital for a month. If you don't walk out of the hospital after this time, you're coming out in a box. Though the grass ticks primarily live in the forests, it's not uncommon for them to set up camp in areas of the city too. If ever I walked near grass Nastya would shout 'Are you stupid?' before rubbing my legs up and down, and checking behind my ears. Apparently if a tick is found pre-bite, it cannot simply be crushed onto your skin, it has to be burned. If however it has taken its first bite, the only way is to pour oil on the wound, which annoys the tick and makes it release itself from your flesh, and then you can pry it out with tweezers.

Although the possibility of being eaten by bears or poisonous insects was very real, when I walked around the city I wasn't inhibited by it. Described by Chekhov as the most beautiful city in Siberia, Krasnoyarsk had a lot to live up to. From wherever you stand you can see mountains, which are almost always snowcapped except for the hundred or so days of summer, and when they are not covered in snow they are a striking dark green from the thousands of trees that live on them. The city centre itself is quite attractive, made up of wide streets and wooden houses from the Stalin years with ornate carvings and window shutters. Although there are a few chain stores, most of the shops are completely unique and are usually quite small. The city is never overly busy, is a peaceful place to walk, and is made especially romantic by the classical music that is played through speakers on lamp posts throughout the day. These speakers were installed during World War II and were used continuously, right through till 1991 when President Mikhail Gorbachev's negotiations with Reagan officially ended the cold war.

Trams still operate throughout and even the old-fashioned second-hand buses from neighbouring countries add to the city's charm, though the traffic was the most obvious example of the Russian class divide. Oligarchs and officials drove around in large off-road vehicles, silver Japanese Mitsubishi 4x4s or ~~American~~ US Humvees while regular people drove cheap Japanese saloons or old Russian cars. I saw an inordinate number of Ladas from the 1970s and 1980s and an occasional sleek vintage car from the 1950s. The majority of vehicles I saw were old, and many had parts missing from small accidents, which are quite common as most people drive like nutcases.

Boris's car was quite old, and Nataliya Petrovna was forever nagging him to buy a new one because it seemed every other day he had to spend an afternoon with his car in the garage because it failed to start. Although this would have driven me crazy, Boris didn't seem to mind. He has an attitude of 'If it's not broken, why replace it?' Which I could understand, but at the same time, his car may not have been broken, but it was on its last legs. Materialism and capitalism are very much looked down upon, not only within my Siberian family, but throughout Krasnoyarsk. Having spoken with some of Nastya's friends, the general view is that 'the soul is more important than money.' Dima, who is aware that I am writing this told me that he hopes it brings me success, 'Not lots of money, but happiness, and a little money.'

I was surprised by the number of people I spoke to who lamented the dissolution of the USSR. One person even attributed its loss, not to the cold war but to Coca-Cola. Although Pepsi was available in the Soviet Union from 1979, Coca-Cola only became available there after the cold war in 1992. This person's theory was that the cost of the cold war resulted in massive economic decline, leading to extreme poverty. This, coupled with the broadcasting of ~~American~~ US television programmes in which seemingly well-off people lived happily and drank Coca-Cola, seduced many of the people in the smaller countries that formed the Soviet Union into thinking they would be better off in a capitalist state; which of course proved not to be the case. Since the dissolution of the Soviet Union, the economies of many former Soviet countries, such as Georgia, and Tajikistan are worse than in 1991, while other former Soviet countries are only marginally improved. Coca-Cola therefore is seen here as a seductive mistress who promises gold but only provides fool's gold.

When I first arrived in Krasnoyarsk, I felt some sort of culture shock, and while being unable to buy welsh cakes, laverbread, or (real) sausages and (real) mashed potato in gravy, I took to buying Coca-Cola, even though I do not drink it normally. I had to keep it a secret however as whenever Boris saw a bottle of it around, he would look at me disapprovingly, say the words 'Cola, bad', and promptly pour it down the toilet. Although Boris wasn't a fan of the Soviets he still lives in the way he had to during their rule. Everything is recycled, including every plastic bottle, scraps of clothing and discarded bits of wood. This is a stark contrast to how the younger Russian generations live. Influenced by capitalist values, the younger people I met liked to have new things, and didn't mind replacing things when they weren't broken. This juxtaposition in attitudes is no clearer than in the city centre, where babushkas live in old wooden buildings that are sandwiched in between contemporary apartment buildings.

At the very centre of the city stands an unfinished, twenty-four storey tower block, the unofficial symbol of Krasnoyarsk. Begun in 1985, the tower was originally constructed to house new businesses, as if Russia somehow knew the transition to capitalism was inevitable. With the subsequent dissolution of the Soviet Union, the tower was abandoned. In the decades since then it has changed hands many times but has never been completed. Today it stands a hollow shell of concrete legs, half glazed with tinted panels. It is a constant reminder of one of the worst recessions Russia has known, and perfectly symbolises the current economic and political climate here. Locked in perpetual recovery, forever unfinished, the tower represents the ever present conflict between capitalist and communist ideals. Construction of the tower block began just before perestroika, the political movement for reformation within the communist party during the 1980s, spearheaded by Mikhail Gorbachev. This was also the period in which Gorbachev sought to introduce glasnost, a policy that called for increased openness and transparency in government institutions. With the building constantly open to the elements while under permanent reconstruction, it seems to perfectly encapsulate Gorbachev's political ideals, though I don't think a half-complete tower was exactly what he had in mind when planning Russia's reform.

People are People

The vast expanse of the Yenisei River makes Krasnoyarsk one of the most pleasant places in the entire world, and even though the city itself is huge, because of all the greenery throughout the suburbs and the centre, and a constant view of the mountains, it always feels to me that I am in a small town. It's not just the old Stalinist architecture, the classical music in the street, the river; the outstanding natural beauty, or the feeling of being miles from the capital and its pseudo capitalist ways; Krasnoyarsk would be nothing without its people.

Nastya told me that when I arrive in Moscow, to blend in well I should pull the meanest face I can and never smile: 'No one smiles in Moscow'. People do tend to look either angry or completely miserable. Before I visited Siberia, my view of Russians came from clichés in films and was that they were mostly crazy, devious, calculating, treacherous people who hated the West, and were likely to be used as spies if they ever went to the UK or ~~America~~ USA. I suppose some people may be. You get crazy devious people wherever you go, but I have never met any in Moscow or Siberia. In fact, I am ashamed now to even think of my Hollywood-instilled notion of Russians. The people I have spoken to in Moscow were kind and open, and the people of Krasnoyarsk even more so. I tend to think of it in terms of the London/Cardiff difference. I have met many foreign travellers in Cardiff, most of whom preferred the people of Wales – Cardiff in particular – to the people of London and England. Not to say they thought the English unkind, just slightly more abrasive than the Welsh.

Siberian people are a world away from the Moscow-dwelling Muscovites. For a start, they smile more often. It's not uncommon to be invited to dinner and be presented with half a dozen courses of meat dishes and vegetables, and to be given some for the way home. Even if you visit someone very briefly they usually put an array of nibbles on the table for you to dip into. They care about other people's wellbeing, as if everyone were distantly related. I have my own theory that this is implanted by two major factors. The first factor is that most Siberian people are poor in monetary terms. Those I have met have little compared to Western standards, and therefore there is an attitude of 'We are all in it together. So why not share'.

The second factor that informs my theory is that Krasnoyarsk is zek country. Krasnoyarsk housed a large number of Gulags – the enforced labour camps of the Stalin era from the 1930s to the 1950s. When the prisoners, known as zeks, were released (if they managed to survive), they couldn't always obtain resident permits for the towns and cities they once lived in and so became residents of Siberia. Not only that but once a prisoner was released, after suffering hard labour in 40° C summers and -40° C winters, they were probably in no state to travel far, and didn't feel they could always be understood by Russians who had not been enslaved themselves. This was something Aleksandr Solzhenitsyn touched on in *The Gulag Archipelago*. According to Solzhenitsyn, there was an understanding between zeks that could not be penetrated or understood by outsiders. This train of thought seems to be apparent even today. The people of Krasnoyarsk and its neighbouring cities have a precious and very rare sense of community, based on hardship, which they know most Westerners cannot fathom. This is something akin to the sense of community I know exists in Ely, Cardiff. However, that community is largely constructed of working class people, some of whom receive state-funded benefits (like my family did). These benefits are seen as a luxury among Siberians, although they do have a slightly less generous welfare system of their own. Having been rescued from drowning myself by Jobseeker's Allowance, even though I hated doing it, and there was a stigma attached to it, I am ever thankful that Britain is still a welfare state. It's a terrible thing that this is currently under attack from the Tory government; if I hadn't been able to float on JSA for a short period between jobs I may have perished, due to a lack of survival skills and an obvious lack of ability and space to grow my own food.

In Siberia, if you don't work, or grow your own food, or you're not an oligarch, you face extreme poverty, unless helped by another. You'd think in a place like Siberia where the weather systems are lethal, the danger of being killed by a number of deadly creatures is very real, and the economic climate is so severe, that only the tough would survive. This is true in a way, because Siberian people are tough, but the conditions set by the weather and the government only strengthen their resolve and their sense of humanity further. Like the people of Ely, Siberians seem to have a greater empathy for those who have it hard. For example: when I was waiting for a bus one day I noticed a babushka crossing the road where there was no designated crossing area. She got halfway across and then stopped because traffic was heavy in both directions. I thought she was going to get killed, but then a large, white off-road car stopped right next to her. The driver parked his vehicle in such a way as to stop the flow of traffic in the two lanes behind him. He got out and walked the woman across to the pavement safely. Then got back in his car and went on his way. It's the little kindnesses that count and Krasnoyarsk is the world's capital of little kindnesses.

Knowing Where to Walk

During that first month in Russia I felt afraid, I was visibly scared of everything and it was noticeable. Though I was never in any danger, the outside world felt so alien, so completely different from what I was used to in Wales, that I interpreted it as being hostile. The apartment blocks, tall and grey, sometimes had balconies that looked as if they were going to fall off and there were many wild dogs that although thin, were agile and obviously hungry. People spoke a language I couldn't understand, and sometimes in very harsh tones, and I didn't know the Cyrillic alphabet. I couldn't even translate the simplest warnings on the buses, or anywhere else. Plus, the fonts used on some of the signs looked decidedly military. Although these things aren't necessarily intimidating, the lack of control I felt was. I had no way of communicating with anyone other than Nastya and I had no control over what I ate either. Nastya did the cooking because I didn't know any of their cooking methods, and as I didn't have a lot of money I couldn't buy my own food. Not only that but it would have been offensive to cook my own meals. At times when we went to a supermarket, Nastya would scorn me for choosing something she said was unhealthy, but at the same time, she would buy a lot of <u>candies</u>. This lack of control over nearly every aspect of my life, at times, drove me further into myself.

Yank Speak

With no spoken Russian at all, I had to be accompanied by Nastya at all times. She was my guide, translator and wife, and the three roles were occasionally too much for her. When she had to work a twelve-hour night shift, I was stuck in the apartment on my own. At times I felt a bit like a prisoner, although I was a prisoner of my own making. Some nights Nataliya Petrovna would come over to cook for me when Nastya was working, but this only made things worse. As we couldn't communicate, I resigned myself to staying in our bedroom with the door closed. When it was time to eat, Nataliya Petrovna would knock on the door and motion me towards the kitchen. Though it was very kind of her to do this, I would rather have been left to my own devices and cooked something myself; there are only so many meatballs one can eat, and as they were home-made, I often found myself crunching teeth against pieces of bone. Even when I was alone at night, it was very difficult to prepare a meal. Many of the food stuffs in the fridge were out of date, and I couldn't tell what a lot of it was. If something had mould on it, they kept it for use in some soup or stew. I was from a culture of 'If it's got green on it, don't risk it', living among a people whose ethos was the opposite.

Alone at night, it was also hard for me to sleep. A massive electricity station stood just across from the apartment on the side of our bedroom and it gave off an electric hum that couldn't be stopped, even with the window closed. Sometimes in the dead of night, this substation released what can only be described as massive explosions, caused by surges in power. These never failed to startle me from sleep, and when several explosions went off in a single night, I had the impression of being alive in a war zone.

On days when Nastya was free we would take walks along the Yenisei or visit whatever attractions were available. There are two Ferris wheels on the north side of the river, one in the park opposite the office where Nastya works and one in the central city park opposite Revolution Square. These wheels never stop turning all year round, except for the holidays around New Year.

About 20ft from each Ferris wheel was the ticket office, where a woman sat inside from morning till night. I couldn't help but feel sorry for her, or for the hundreds of other people like her in similar roles. Spread all over the city there are tiny little shops, some no bigger than ice cream vans. There is no access inside them except for a backdoor which is always locked. These kiosks are product specific. They either sell magazines, ice cream or cigarettes. There are more cigarette kiosks than any other. Each stall has just one person inside. Outside of these you tend to see two or three Coca-Cola-branded fridges of the type you find in British corner shops. The difference in Russia is that these fridges stand in the street and can only be opened by the stall keeper who, once she has taken your money, pushes a button that remotely releases the magnetic lock on the fridge door. She then watches as you take exactly what you paid for.

I thought it ironic that the ice cream kiosks were full of electrically operated freezers, even though it was below freezing outside. The person inside each had an electric heater too. It's a great shame that they don't stand outside in winter and store their ice creams in the snow, they would probably save a fortune on electricity, but I guess it would be a really uncomfortable way to make a living. Still people do it. Along the roadsides between our home and Nastya's office there were many people sat on stools. They had little trays in front of them, some of which had a few potatoes, some a few berries. These people, who were no doubt officially retired, would spend their whole days sitting there in the cold, trying to sell a few items they had grown at their dachas, in order to top up their small pensions. Near our apartment stood a row of shops, and outside these shops it was normal to see rusty cars parked up with the boot open. Inside the boot lay a range of red meats I could only assume was deer, laid down on pieces of torn carpet. Sometimes they even presented their stock on the bonnet. The people stood next to these cars never approached anyone or called out their prices. They just hung around, cold, wrapped up in several tattered coats, waiting for someone to ignore the shops perhaps and inquire after cheaper meats.

Apart from the street sellers and kiosks there are several larger shops that range in size and quality. Firstly, there are small convenient stores that are attached to residential blocks, taking up the space where a ground floor flat would be. These shops are unique in that you can't simply walk in and pick up the things you want, when you enter the store you walk into what can only be described as a large cage. In these shops you have to know what you want, ask for it, pay for it through a small square opening in the bars and take your goods from the same place. Awkward if you have a long list of things you want or if you can't speak Russian.

The supermarkets are a different affair altogether. They are very similar to their UK cousins; however, when you enter, if you have any bags with you, you must lock them away in one of the many lockers provided near the till points. They have most of the same products you can find in the West; however they do range greatly in quality and cost. Some sell much better meat products than others, but what they all have in common is that many products are out of date. This makes shopping even more tiresome because it becomes a quest to find the products you want that are the least past their use by date. My theory is that while many people in Russia grow food on their own plots of land, having become dependent on these plots after the fall of the Soviet Union, supermarkets have no choice but to keep selling out-of-date stock because people just don't buy it fast enough.

When it was just the two of us, we had to do some kind of supermarket shopping to avoid using the out-of-date products in the fridge. One evening, while in the middle of cooking, we decided to go to a supermarket near Nastya's office. It was a Friday evening and the streets were full of drunken Russian men. We weren't accosted or spoken to on our way there as all the drunken people were either too busy enjoying themselves to notice us or they had fallen asleep on the street.

Once we had our goods, Nastya led me to another main road that could also take us home. Not only would it have made our journey shorter but there would likely be fewer drunken people. When we approached the road it was pitch dark. Because of the lack of shops of any kind it hadn't been fitted with street lamps. Halfway down we could see a police car with two militia sat there quietly. Nastya began to walk back, appearing as if she had taken a wrong turning. She explained that though they could be decent people, and I had my passport in my pocket, complete with immigration card and registration, they could stop us if they wanted to, ignore the fact I had my papers in order and attempt to get a bribe. It was safer to go back the way we came.

Khrushchev's Permanent Thaw

Russian apartments are noticeably different from those I have known in the UK in that they are usually confined to one floor and are made with the same love and care that the buildings are made with. Instead of skirting boards, many floors have lino, which is cut in such a way that it rides up the wall three inches on all sides and bunches up in the corners. Paint is used sparingly – many ceilings in Russia are covered in those horrible polystyrene tiles with coving made of the same material, and the wallpaper is badly fitted. Nearly every joint of paper overlaps the other. In places where a wall meets a cupboard and there is a gap that would normally be disguised with a wooden panel in the UK, they simply apply a badly cut strip of wallpaper over it. These often peel slightly and so small holes are usually visible around cupboards, and there are many cupboards. Any void above a doorway is usually turned into a cupboard. In this way Russian apartments are similar to submarines – every inch of space counts.

To counter the poor standard of decoration, Nataliya Petrovna had hung pictures wherever she could, only none of the frames matched or seemed in keeping with the colour of the walls. Some pictures were even without frames and were simply pinned to the wall. There was also little evidence of personal possessions. Nobody seemed to own much of anything. Looking at other peoples apartments, it became clear that this was typical of most Russians. With the exception of a few fridge magnets and pictures on walls there is very little of anything in any apartment to give an indication as to who lives there. I got the impression that people primarily concerned themselves with objects that were of use. My mother would have cried. As the world's most finicky and house-proud woman, she would have had a fit had she seen it. None of the furniture matched or the walls and curtains. It may sound silly, but as a twenty-eight-year-old man, who has lived in countless rented rooms, and has never really given much thought to furniture or wallpaper, it even jarred with me. Because my dad's a builder we had had to suffer stacks of tools and various 'might come in handy later' bits-n-bobs, but still, my mother hoovered every day and would never let a guest enter if the house wasn't perfect. I think I have inherited her genes. Either that or I have inherited my father's; my father who is known for being a perfectionist in his building work, and therefore a real pain to work for. When laying new wooden floors my dad always insisted on using scrim cloths before varnishing. I remember speaking to a working eighty-four-year-old builder mate of my dad in one of the buildings they were fixing. When I had asked him about working for my dad, he said 'Your dad uses scrim cloths. Scrim cloths to dust surfaces after they've been brushed with a duster. Nobody uses them anymore; even I never even used 'em when I was twenty.' So as the son of Wales's fussiest builder, and a hoover-crazy mother, Nastya's parents' apartment was a slight shock to the system.

However, like the house I grew up in, all the cupboards above the doors, and the balcony leading off from the living room were filled with Boris's things: spare car parts, old shoes with worn soles, and jars of 'might come in handy one day'. In the living room, against the left wall, stood a large, brown laminated unit typical of the 1960s, that spanned the whole length. Through the glass panels I could see at least fifty books. Other sections without a glass front were filled with more of Boris's gear and spare parts, and one glass-fronted section had its glass covered with silver foil to prevent anyone seeing the piles of spare machinery parts inside. I later learned this is something Nataliya Petrovna had forced Boris to do as she felt ashamed at guests seeing so many of Boris's dirty tools. The only item that truly reflected Nataliya Petrovna's personality was a large black Enisei piano that stood against the wall opposite from the one with the large brown unit. She'd had musical training and had come from relatively good beginnings.

Towards the last two weeks of my visit, Nastya's parents kept appearing unexpectedly and would often stay the night. They slept in the living room, which is where they had slept most nights since Baba Ira moved in roughly fifteen years earlier. This may sound strange to some people but it was something I was used to before coming to Russia. Growing up with three sisters in a two-bedroom house, my parents actually slept in the living room until their divorce. As a teenager, this was something that had annoyed me as I couldn't stay up late and watch TV, or walk through the living room to the kitchen without waking up my parents. Similarly, in Krasnoyarsk, I couldn't walk to the balcony at night for a smoke, which was the only place permitted; but it felt cosy, like it had when I was a small boy. One of my fondest memories is coming home from a school trip at the age of seven. We had been to the dinosaur exhibition in Cardiff Museum, and I had bought a plastic woolly mammoth. As the trip finished at about midday, when I got home, my parents, who had decided to have a lie-in, were still in their blankets on the living-room floor. I woke them up and showed them my new toy. It was quite lovely being able to walk through the front door and find them sleeping. I suppose Nastya would have similar memories, only in hers she would have gone to the Krasnoyarsk Museum, which had an actual woolly mammoth in it.

Occasionally the sky was so bleak and snow-laden it was as if it contained all the Sundays of my teenage years. Although it was spring, it was still fairly cold, and we couldn't stay out for too long in the evenings without catching a chill. To pass the time, Nastya and I spent any night she wasn't working watching British sitcoms in the permanent warmth of home. Usually, after about four hours of *The IT Crowd,* we were so bored that we would go to sit in the kitchen for a change of atmosphere. With Nastya's help I sometimes plucked up the courage to ask Nataliya Petrovna about the family's history.

When the USSR collapsed in 1991, hyperinflation left many starving to death. People famously queued down the street for a loaf of bread or some milk. Nataliya Petrovna and Boris, who both worked for the energy company, had to continue working for three years without pay until the economy began to recover. They continued working without pay as the company still paid for their apartment, the utility bills and Nastya's and Dima's musical tuition. This was normal under the Soviet remuneration system and continued until the country stabilised once more. Had they stopped working, they would have lost their pensions, the apartment and dacha; all of which were crucial to their survival. During this period of instability, at least two of Nataliya Petrovna's friends and work colleagues drank themselves to death. The Semenov family would have starved if it weren't for Boris's hunting skills.

It was clear from the start that Boris and his wife were very different from each other. Boris, who had originated from a small hunting village in the Evenkiyskiy district a few hundred miles west of Krasnoyarsk, came to the city as an engineer and worked at the same energy plant for his entire career until retirement. Although he was a member of modern civilised society Boris never left his hunting roots behind. At any and every opportunity he goes hunting or spends his time preparing for hunting trips. Boris has a vast amount of equipment that is spread throughout the apartment, dacha and a garage he owns. Because of the way he has lived his life, and the mountains he climbs regularly, his physique is something to be in awe of. He put me to shame. In fact he would put most people to shame, including a large percentage of athletes.

When Boris was in the apartment he would sit at the kitchen table and repair things. Because of his age and failing eyesight, he would wear goggles that looked a lot like a cross between a welder's mask and a jeweller's eyepiece. Even when he wasn't fixing something, he would walk around with them still on his head, making him resemble a mad professor. Boris makes a lot of his own equipment or modifies things he buys. His headlamp has several different lenses and a home-made battery unit. His backpacks are enlarged and home-sewn. When Nastya and I came home, we would often find Boris sat at the old-fashioned sewing table in the hallway making some new bag for carrying meat. On two occasions, I have seen a glimpse of his gun, a semi-automatic Kalashnikov rifle that looked modified to the extent that it appeared home-made. This weapon was never left lying around but kept in a locked steel box somewhere in the storeroom next to the bathroom. I only saw it when Boris was checking it over for his next hunting trip.

With his education as a technical engineer Boris is good at making and repairing most things; especially his car. When his previous vehicle died a death, he bought the exact same model from a second-hand dealer and used his dead car as parts to make the new one like new. When Boris wasn't sitting at the sewing table or the kitchen table with his goggles on he would fall asleep on the living room sofa and snore loudly. Looking at him, it was like watching a sleeping beast. For although Boris is very mild mannered and loves to joke, he also has a fiery temper. This, coupled with his perfectly formed body, makes Boris one of the world's deadliest people though I must say that I've never felt intimidated by him. He keeps his temper stored up for when there is a need for it, and there has been occasion it was needed. While out on his hunting trips, Boris has had to face bears and wild cats. He has fought for his life against some the world's greatest and most ferocious creatures, and so far has never lost a fight. Although Boris snores like a beast, whenever I walked past him sleeping I had the sense that he was watching me with hawk eyes. I could never be sure if he was watching me or not, although he gave the impression of sleeping heavily Boris is actually an extremely light sleeper and can spring from slumber into fast action in a second. I suppose this comes from his inherited hunter's awareness and from hundreds of nights sleeping out in the taiga.

For Boris to catch his prey, he has to catch a train heading north carrying anything up to sixty kilos of equipment or more. In his large rucksack, he carries all the potatoes he needs to survive a month in the wild, as well as knives, medicines, and weapons. He also carries a pair of 10 ft home-made skis. These skis are unusual in that they are covered with fur and are longer as well as wider than normal recreational skis. They are essential for travelling in the taiga where snowdrifts can be as high as 15 ft. Without these Boris can't hunt. Once the train has been travelling north for seven hours, Boris disembarks in what seems like the middle of nowhere, and because he always catches a train in early evening he normally arrives in the early hours of the morning when it is pitch black. He then has to hike an hour before reaching a wide and treacherous river. To cross this he has a home-made boat that he keeps buried in the woods. As the river is fast, and very deep, Boris has to use all his strength to paddle his boat and his sixty kilos of gear across to the other side. Once on the other side he then has to hike a few hours to reach his first hut. This hut is in such a remote part of the taiga that it is never disturbed, except by bears. Here he takes as much sleep as he needs before taking a further ten-hour hike to his second hut, which is closer to his hunting ground. Boris can spend as much as a month at this second hut with only himself for company. There is no mobile phone coverage either. If he wants to make a phone call, he has to climb a different mountain to get a small signal. This he does quite often to call Nataliya Petrovna. His calls are never necessary, but he likes to speak to his wife and play jokes. Sometimes he says an earthquake has destroyed his hut and he is sleeping in a tree, or he will say he is being chased by a party of bears with rifles. Anything to amuse.

Nataliya Petrovna, by contrast, is not so physical. She is short and round and not capable of climbing any mountains let alone fighting bears. Unlike Boris, Nataliya Petrovna is very sociable and likes to dress to impress at one of her many dinner parties. When she has guests over, she always makes an effort to look good, by arranging her hair into curls and by wearing dresses. She is as mild mannered as Boris, but flies into a rage if there are hunting things left around for people to trip over. Nataliya Petrovna likes everything put in its proper place and despises dirty things. She also likes to joke around. When Boris telephones from some distant mountain she pretends she is having a great time without him and tells him not to return. After such phone calls, she pines over him and berates herself for having said silly things.

When she is not looking after her grandson Semka, or playing the piano, she is cooking. Her speciality is *golubtsi*. This is meat wrapped in cabbage leaves that must be boiled in an inch of water for an hour and thirty minutes. Nataliya Petrovna knows all there is to know about preparing meat dishes. It is her job to cut up all the meat Boris brings home. When he brings back the limbs of deer Nataliya Petrovna spends many of the evenings after cleaning them – chopping bits, mincing bits in her electric mincer, bagging it, sealing it and storing it away in one of the three freezers. They have a normal fridge-freezer in the kitchen. When this freezer is full she then uses the other much larger freezers in the cupboard next to the bathroom. They are rarely short of good cuts of meat.

With the mincemeat Nataliya Petrovna usually makes *pelmeni* and *manti* (both similar to ravioli). She makes so much *pelmeni* that she very often gives whole bags of it away to friends.

After the collapse of the USSR, and the suicides of several of their friends, Boris brought back so much meat that Nataliya Petrovna made enough *pelmeni* to spread around and keep some of her friends alive. When they were short of something essential Nataliya Petrovna had only to make a call to someone to make a trade in *pelmeni*. It was their primary bargaining tool at a time when money was worthless. If Boris hadn't the skills to hunt, I'm not sure what would have happened to everyone. It's possible Nastya might never have survived. When I sat down with Nastya and her mother and questioned them about the collapse of the Soviet Union, Nataliya Petrovna said: 'I have never been poor, but neither have I ever been rich. No matter who came into power and regardless of communist or capitalist rule, life went on as normal. Not one president, with all the promises they made ever really changed anything.'

Even so, I got the sense that both Nastya's parents missed the earlier part of their lives even though they had lived under Soviet rule. Nataliya Petrovna had been alive no longer than three years when Stalin died, and so grew up under Khrushchev's thaw. Premier Nikita Khrushchev famously denounced Stalin's policies, released millions of Soviet political prisoners from the Gulags and attempted to fully reverse repression and censorship by what became later known as de-Stalinisation. Even with the rise of Brezhnev, who set to work on reversing Khrushchev's reforms, many of the cultural reforms proved irreversible. Khrushchev's policy changes made it possible for the likes of the Shurik movies to be made. Played by Aleksandr Demyanenko, Shurik, with his bleached-blond hair and thick-rimmed glasses, became a recurrent character in slapstick comedies of the 1960s and early 1970s. His movies, which epitomise the sixties in Russia, are still shown regularly today. In fact, during my first month in Russia, I saw them all, more than once.

With the sounds of the sixties coming from the TV, and the typical view of Soviet residential blocks from the window I sometimes felt as though we were still living in the Khrushchev period. This sense of being lost in the past was broken every evening by a neighbour, who would pull up at the foot of the building in his souped-up sports car playing Vangelis' 'Conquest of Paradise' as loud as his speakers would allow. Which was quite appropriate as that song was recorded just after the fall of the USSR.

The Red Army Strikes

Russian bread was something else I had to get used to. There were few of the factory-made thick, medium or thin sliced loaves that come in plastic wrappers. Instead loaves of bread come in various irregular shapes; they never last more than three days and always taste very good. The size of the loaf we bought depended on how many people were at home at the time, as waste is sorely frowned on. To play safe Nastya and I normally bought a miniature unsliced loaf every day. During meal times everyone got a slice of bread, even if the meal was meat and potatoes or fish pie. Though they weren't exactly slices as I had known them, more like one-third-of-a-slice, the same size you would use for egg and soldiers. At first I thought that this was ritual behavior, leftover from times of hardship but in actual fact Russians are just really fond of eating bread with everything. They eat it with chicken, they eat it with rice, with any and every dish you really wouldn't think of accompanying with bread, they have a slice or two. When I was on the first flight to Russia, there had been a soldier of bread, wrapped in plastic alongside the meal. At first I thought that they were being stingy, but later, when I got settled in the apartment, I understood it was normal practice.

One evening, while eating meatballs and home-made mashed potato with the obligatory slice of bread, Nataliya Petrovna told me the story of her grandfathers. Following the October Revolution of 1917, Nataliya Petrovna's paternal grandfather, Fyodor Rosov – who was a geologist and a man of means – fled Russia with his brother Ivan. According to her story, neither man had any particular political ideology but as they were both accustomed to a decent standard of living they feared assassination by the Red Army. People from wealthy backgrounds were being slaughtered left right and centre, so the only option for them was to leave. They fled via the Black Sea for Turkey, made their way to Tunisia, and eventually settled in France. I later did some research on this subject and found that their exile from Russia had been documented in one of Moscow's museums, Marina Tsvetaeva. According to the museum, Ivan, brother to Fyodor Rozov, studied law at Yekaterinburg University and was mobilised into the white army in 1918 where he graduated to Midshipman in the Black Sea Fleet. He later settled in Reims where he worked as a driver and in 1953 became a priest and founded the Church of the Assumption of Oni in 1954.

Little is known about Fyodor. What we do know is that when Fyodor fled for Turkey with his brother, he left behind a pregnant wife, Marina Rosova, Nataliya Petrovna's grandmother. Apparently Marina (who was pregnant with Nataliya Petrovna's father at the time, the unborn son of a 'white deserter'), was so beautiful that the Red Army couldn't bring themselves to kill her, as was their custom when they came across the wives of 'traitors of Russia'. She later married Anton Karbovski, a high-ranking Cheka (secret policeman) of the NKVD (The People's Commissariat for Internal Affairs). He was so in love with Marina that, against regulation, he located all documents that gave evidence of her original marriage and destroyed them, so she would not be exterminated during any of the purges. Marina gave birth to Pyotr Karbovski, who grew up to become loyal to the communist party, and the NKVD. When Pyotr came of age he was contacted by his biological father, through his Aunt in St Petersburg. Pyotr, being a devout communist, reported all of these letters to the NKVD who said that if he never replied to Fyodor, he could continue life exactly as he had already. In those times, when one applied for work, a questionnaire had to be filled out that asked if you had relatives abroad. Pyotr had always stated that he hadn't and under the advice of the NKVD continued to do so even though his natural father was alive and well in France.

In 1941, Pyotr was studying engineering at the University of Yekaterinburg when war broke out. He volunteered for the war effort and was sent by train to Moscow. However he never made it to Moscow. Halfway through the journey the train stopped for supplies and Pyotr got off to beg some hot water somewhere nearby. The train then departed leaving him behind. This was classed as treachery. As punishment he was sent to the front line as part of the strafnoi battalion. His job was a suicide mission: advance, advance, advance and never turn back. The NKVD he had so devoutly admired were now fifty paces behind him all the way, with machine guns at his back. Pyotr was not expected to survive, but was saved by the severely cold winter of 1941. He got frostbitten on several of his toes. Once these were amputated he was classed as an invalid and sent back to Yekaterinburg, where he continued his studies in university and met his future wife, Iraida Furtaeva (Ira). Nine years later Iraida gave birth to a daughter, Nataliya Petrovna Karbovskaya, my mother-in-law.

Aeroflot Flight SU0241. April 16th 2011. Moscow — London

After a long and tearful goodbye I was once again alone and lonely on a plane full of Russians. Before my adventure I had made plans for one trip, and one trip only, as if I was going on some holiday that also included a wedding. The fact was that the wedding had been my own, and as a married man I had to get my head out of the clouds and think seriously about where life was heading and what I needed to do.

As the plane ascended into the sky, and I looked down on Moscow, it became clear that I had not only married a woman, but an entire country. My life, as I had known it, would never be the same again, which was both a good and a bad thing. There were countless things I would miss in the UK: people, places, foods and so on but it was too late to turn back the clock. I didn't want to anyway. I was now half-Welsh, half-Russian. Nastya would be waiting for me as she had done ever since Paris. It broke my heart to think of the way she had cried in Moscow. To think of all the nights we would have to spend apart; but it couldn't be helped. My visa had expired. And although I hated the thought of it, I had to go back to go forward.

After hoovering up the contents of my inflight meal, and washing it all down with weak aeroplane coffee, I reclined my seat and relaxed. I loathed leaving Nastya behind but at the same time I was relieved to be back in control of myself again. I couldn't wait to get back to the UK and tell my friends all I'd seen, and I'd seen a lot. It felt like such relief to be on my own, to be moving away from Russia, which was no surprise considering what had happened the night before.

Moscow, Fridge Magnets, and Tactical Nuclear Weapons

We arrived in the early morning at Moscow Domededovo Airport, which is south and some considerable distance away from Moscow. To get to the city we bundled ourselves into the back of a minivan along with several other travellers. This is quite normal – taxis are expensive and buses can take a long time to wait for, a bus-taxi cross is the cheaper option because it can carry about ten people, and it runs much faster than the bus service. We were dropped off at the nearest Moscow metro station an hour later. Before we caught the metro to our hostel, I wanted to stand in the street and smoke a cigarette, a Russian cigarette. I wanted to capture the moment, and there is no better way I know of than to stand still and smoke. Moscow looked practically European compared to Krasnoyarsk. The roads were already busy with people on their way to work and the sun was shining against the office blocks; it made me feel like I was back in Paris for a moment.

When we reached our hostel some three hours later, we were both shattered, having travelled through the night, so we bunked down and fell fast asleep. When we awoke it was early evening. The opportunity to see the Tsaritsyno palace had passed us by. There was only enough time left to do some souvenir shopping and have a bite to eat. Moscow is different from Krasnoyarsk in that there are thousands of restaurants of good quality and kiosks in the streets that sell Western style foods. I will never forget that first slice of pizza after a month in Siberia. It was heaven. We didn't stop there however, after several slices of pizza we went to a Turkish restaurant and ate ourselves silly. Our hostel and the restaurant were both on Yamskogo Polya Street near the

Belorusskaya train station. We had chosen to stay at that hostel precisely because it was so near to it. The shuttle train to Sheremetyevo Airport would leave from there the following morning.

As the evening was descending quickly, we decided to walk to Belorusskaya to make sure we knew the fastest route and because it was likely there would be shops that sold tourist pap. We needed to buy a fridge magnet for my mum and some Soviet chocolate for my dad. To get to the station, we first had to ascend some concrete steps that lead to Leningradsky Avenue. This road is raised as it has to pass over the Moskva-Smolenskaya Railway line. When we reached Leningradsky there were hundreds of people gathered there. They were waiting for something and obviously had knowledge that we didn't, so we waited with them. A fleet of orange street-cleaning vehicles came and began washing the road. They were only cleaning the stretch of road that was visible to us. There must have been twenty of them. They took it in turns to run in relays and it took about half an hour to wash just a 200-metre stretch, as the road was nine lanes wide. During this time militia came. Not the normal street militia, but highly decorated officers. Many of them walked along the edge of the pavement and took up positions by the side of the road as a preventative measure to stop people stepping out. They didn't have to say anything as people naturally backed away from them.

When the road was clean, and the militia were in place, we watched in silence as tanks came screaming through, hundreds of them, with soldiers popping up slightly through the turrets. These were followed by a range of military vehicles including mobile surface-to-air rocket launchers, each equipped with no fewer than sixteen barrels. When at least a hundred heavy-armoured tanks, rocket launchers and various killing machines had sped by, we asked a Muscovite what it was all about. We were told that the killing machines we had seen were just a practice run for Victory Day, which is held on May 9th. This display of military might is to celebrate the day Nazi Germany surrendered to the Soviet Union and its allies in 1945. Having seen some footage of Moscow's military parades before I came to Russia I knew that something was missing. There was no way any kind of military display, even on a practice run, would finish with tanks. I knew something much bigger was coming. The militia and throngs of people prevented me from getting a decent view of the road so I urged Nastya to follow me past Belorusskaya station to the junction where Leningradsky Avenue meets Leningradsky Prospekt. All the vehicles we had seen so far had not travelled the length of the avenue and so I deduced that they must have come from the road next to it. I was right.

When we got to the junction a huge, sixteen-wheeled, fully-armed nuclear weapon launcher was negotiating the corner of Leningradsky Avenue. There were three more behind it. During some later research I found that this machine is known as the Topol-M intercontinental ballistic missile launcher, which carries a single warhead with an 800 kiloton yield (as a comparison the bombs dropped on Hiroshima and Nagasaki were 15 and 21 kilotons respectively). It is quite simply the Godfather of killing machines, and I was stood 10 ft from a convoy of them.

Easter in the Dacha

On Sunday 24th April, the day before we left for Moscow, it was Easter Sunday and there would be no escaping the festivities. In Russia, Easter is celebrated for the same reasons as in Britain – it is a religious holiday, but many people just use it as an excuse to gather with friends and family for a piss-up, much like my family did back in the UK. The snow had receded enough for us to visit the family dacha on the outskirts of the city in the Pugachevo district. Nobody seemed quite sure if I would ever be in Russia again and they wanted me to taste life the old way. Dachas are wooden summerhouses, and our family's dacha was built by Boris and his father-in-law's father, in a district for energy workers only. This was normal practice under the Soviet remuneration system. When someone worked full time in communist Russia, the company you worked for granted you a plot of land on which to build your house and paid certain bills for you.

Each dacha district has a gate, which is usually open, as they aren't much of a deterrent to thieves when all the fences are wire or wooden slats. Almost every dacha in the area had a sticker on it with the year on, showing that they had paid their annual security fee of a few hundred roubles. Every dacha district has in it a small hut where security men spend their whole days waiting for trouble. Paying the security fee is not essential when you own a dacha; however it is such a small price to pay someone to watch over your property. Those who do not pay the fee apparently get broken into more often as the security man is obliged to ignore it. However Nastya told me that everyone suspected that those who didn't pay the fee were broken into by the very security officials paid to protect that area, because they were disgruntled over losing money.

Walking into the dacha felt like walking into the very stereotype of Russia I thought I would have encountered on my first day. With the exception of a few mod cons – sockets, light fittings, a sink and an old fridge-freezer – the dacha fulfilled every preconceived idea I had of Siberian living. When I first sat down and studied my surroundings, what stood out most of all was the large white fridge. Against the dark wood behind, it seemed really out of place. When Boris saw me looking at it, he exclaimed in perfect English 'Soviet manufacture. Good make.'

Boris had built his dacha well. The ground floor has several rooms including the washroom and dining room, which had been added later as an extension. To enter the heart of the dacha you have first to enter the extension, and then walk through what would have been the original entrance, a very solid and heavy pine door. In the original section of the dacha, the biggest bulk is made of pine trunks, sawn down the length and knitted together. It is the most solid structure I have ever seen. At its centre is a fireplace, which acts as a stove. This is made from brick, and the chimney continues right through the centre of the second floor to the roof. On the ground floor, this stove acts as a natural divide between the lower bedroom and original kitchen/dining area. The upper floor, which has the chimney acting as a pillar in the centre, is the master bedroom. The chimney column is unlike those I have seen in the UK. In order to trap heat, instead of being built vertically, it first snakes around itself before towering up into the ceiling. Even though there are two designated sleeping places, there are seven beds in the dacha. There are so many places to sleep as Russians like to live in their dachas from spring until the end of August and they love to receive guests there and have people stay over. Russian hospitality is almost a hobby in itself. Russians genuinely love having people come to visit them, they love to wine and dine people, and they love to offer their guests warm beds at night, only to cook a big breakfast in the morning, and see their guests off with arms full of food for the way home.

Our Easter celebration resembled more of a medieval feast. There were huge plates and trays covered with pork, beef, deer, chicken and potatoes. Nataliya Petrovna had served several bowls of salad with hard-boiled eggs that had intricate colourful designs on their shells. We were joined by several of Nataliya Petrovna's friends and everyone ate heartily. There were several toasts made to Easter and my marriage to Nastya, using several bottles of vodka and cognac, though nobody got drunk. This is because of what I refer to as Russian vodka etiquette. Firstly, vodka can only be drunk from a small glass named a *stopka*; this is to ensure that the vodka is pure and not dirtied by lesser spirits. True to stereotype most Russians can and do drink enough vodka to kill a dinosaur, but after each shot they eat a slice of cucumber, tomato or a slice of Russian sausage called smoked *kolbasa*. This sausage is nothing like the pink sausage meat I had eaten in Moscow. Smoked *kolbasa* is exceptionally tasty and there are hundreds of variations of it. Because it can last a long time in the open, it's also a good meat to take with you on long-distance trips. If there is no salad or sausage left, Russians will pick at anything after a shot of vodka; a spoonful of soup or a slice of bread all help to neutralise the initial effect of the alcohol. This technique keeps Russians from getting blind drunk. In summertime, instead of cucumbers, Russians like to follow vodka with a slice of melon and can get through several in one evening.

This was the first time I had drunk vodka since I was fifteen. I had actually been dreading it. Back in the early nineties, my sister Mab and I had been close. When my parents were in the beginning stages of their very lengthy and horrendously noisy divorce, Mab left to study English at university, leaving me to fend for myself. On the rare times she visited, we would normally stay up all night and share stories. Knowing I was no stranger to alcohol, during one of her visits, Mab introduced me to vodka. We sat up all night watching the original *Star Wars* films on a small television, doing shots mixed with lemonade. This was great, and I remember it fondly, right up to the point the lemonade ran out. My only memory after that was throwing up my spaghetti hoops. I learned later that Mab had cleaned up after me, though she never mentioned it, ever. Sat in the dacha, looking at the bottles of vodka, knowing I wouldn't be able to refuse, only my sister, thousands of miles away could have possibly understood my trepidation. I followed each shot with half a cucumber, and all was well.

After our meal, Nastya wanted to show me the local lake. Russia is covered with thousands of natural lakes that vary greatly in size. The one nearest the dacha is about the size of a school playing field. To reach it you have to walk down a very steep stony path that is flanked by long blades of grass. Though the lake itself isn't much to look at, it was hard to take my eyes off it. The water was murky, there were reeds all around the edge, and it was covered in water skates; but with the sky mirrored, it was a very welcome patch of blue among the dark green of the trees encompassing it. For just beyond the lake, past a handful of dachas, was the taiga.

Aeroflot Flight SU781. July 20th 2011. Moscow — Krasnoyarsk

My family back in Wales hadn't taken the news of my Siberian marriage too badly. Both my mother and father had suspected I was having some sort of clandestine relationship, and I had already told my sisters that I was planning to marry just before I'd left on my first trip. I hadn't mentioned anything of Nastya to my parents beforehand for two very good reasons. Firstly, everything I say I'm going to do I end up not doing. Like the Sahara Desert Marathon I told everyone I was going to run when I reached my twenty-fifth birthday, and the numerous times I said I would quit smoking. If I wanted something to work I had to keep it a secret, otherwise it would be jinxed. When I took up Kung Fu in my early twenties, it was six months before anyone found out. Knowing my tendency to make a hash of things after I'd announced my plans to the world, I had no choice but to keep everyone in the dark over Nastya. The second reason for keeping mum was that I already had a string of failed relationships trailing behind me. I knew exactly what my family would have said if I'd told them 'I'm seeing a girl in Siberia, it's serious and we're going to marry. Honest.' They would have thought I was crazy or laughed their arses off. Some friends of mine (who I had confessed to before my marriage) had joked that I was buying myself a Russian bride because I couldn't satisfy women in Wales. This was rather hurtful, not to mention offensive to Nastya. So, when I saw my family, and revealed all, I was met with the obvious 'What are you going to do now?' To which I replied 'I haven't got a clue.' And I didn't. When making all our plans, Nastya and I hadn't quite reached the part *after* the wedding.

This was quite a difficult time. Nastya and I spoke online most days and discussed options, which was all quite pointless as we didn't have any. We were stuck on a treadmill of the same questions. Could she somehow move to Britain? Could I find a job that paid me £20,000 in a short space of time? Could we possibly move to France? By the end of May I was thoroughly depressed. I spent my days looking for work, pushing for any job I could find, while bunking down each night at one of my parents' places. All the while I was conscious that I had a wife in Siberia, and that we ought to be making plans together. I was in despair at being torn in half by immigration regulations, but at the same time I was happy because I had Nastya and knew that whatever happened, we would be together in the end. By mid-June I had enough money for another tourist visa and a set of return flights. I could have, if I'd wanted, gone to Russia on a longer visa, because I was now part-Russian, but there was a piece of me that was still very much afraid; not only of Russia, but of the massive changes I knew I had to make. Though I was married, my head hadn't caught up with my heart.

I left for Russia on July 1)th with a suitcase half-full of clothes, half-full of ch olates. Our first month had been expensive with Nastya meeting me in Moscow, taking the Trans-Siberian and then returning to Moscow with me. So this time I had to do it alone. Negotiating Sheremetyevo to catch my connecting flight to Krasnoyarsk had been easy as all the signs are in English as well as Russian.

After our plane had descended to a level that allowed us to see everything well from the windows, we had to circle Krasnoyarsk and the surrounding area due to a queue of planes also ready to land. As the frost evaporated from the glass, I got a bird's-eye-view of the hydroelectric power station.

Two weeks after we were married, when the snow began to melt and the grass started showing, Boris had told us that the roads were clear enough to drive far outside the city to visit the hydroelectric power station, also known as Krasnoyarsk dam. The only pictures I had seen of it were on the back of the ten rouble note and a few postcards. At first I was slightly bemused. I'd seen dams before. Surely once you'd seen one you'd seen them all? But I went along as it was something to do, and I had spent too long in the apartment.

Driving to the dam was slightly scary because we had to travel on roads that had been little used through the winter and were still iced over in places. The road ran through a dense forest area. It looked like bear country because it was their country. At the start of our journey, we had to pass through the south side of Krasnoyarsk, which is much older in appearance than the north. The roads on the south side have more potholes and because trams make up a large percentage of the public transport system, we had to drive across railroad tracks every few minutes. I was amazed at how little the south had progressed compared with the north. There were more factories, and the air seemed thicker. It made me glad that we lived on the other side of the river. So many of the buildings looked as if the Second World War had only finished the week before, however, I knew the German invasion hadn't made it so far east. Arriving at the dam wasn't much better. The giant concrete structure could be seen for miles on the approach. In front of the dam was a large glass-fronted building, similar to the residential apartment blocks. It looked like the factory from the beginning of the *Dr Zhivago* movie, where Alec Guinness is looking for his brother's daughter. Next to this was another slightly smaller one. Although less intimidating in size, the smaller building had a giant picture of Vladimir Lenin's face in red and black on its side; a terrifying 50 ft homage to the Communist Party.

I later learned that this dam and its accompanying buildings were partly built by Gulag slaves during the 1950s and were completed just nine years before I was born. It was impossible to get close to the neighbouring buildings, let alone the dam, as a high perimeter fence surrounded the entire complex. This steel fence had a couple of rows of barbed wire on top. When I walked close to it, Nastya and Boris called out in Russian. I couldn't understand what they were saying but I could tell from their tone that they were trying to warn me. Outside the perimeter fence were a few patches of long grass. The snow had melted sufficiently for the deadly Siberian grass ticks to come back; they were waiting for some stupid Westerner to come close. I backed away from the complex and admired its impenetrability. There were a few other tourists there, speaking Russian. One of them managed to get close enough to touch the fence. At that point an electric voice rang out from speakers I hadn't noticed and the man backed away very quickly. They left soon afterwards; which prompted us to follow.

From the plane it didn't look anywhere near as menacing as it had up close. It was impossible to see Lenin, and the big grey buildings looked a lot like one of the residential buildings. If anything, with the great body of water behind it, it was a much better experience to see it from the sky.

PART II

Aeroflot Flight SU778. August 17th 2011. Krasnoyarsk — Moscow

Arriving back in Krasnoyarsk had felt different from the first time, in that it felt like I was returning home. Although the three months I had spent in the UK were busy, I had felt very claustrophobic, which I think had more to do with staying with my parents than anything else. It's not that I felt I had become Siberian or that my life in the UK was awful, but home was wherever my wife was.

Another reason it felt different is because it was summer, and it was this summer that I learned about the Siberia I had never known or heard of back in the UK. In summer most of southern Siberia is exceptionally hot, and the temperature in places can reach the high thirties. Those first few days in the apartment I had to learn how to cope with extreme heat. In place of the shirt, jumper, trousers and thick socks I had worn in the early spring, I now had to wear shorts, t-shirts and flip-flops. I hadn't worn shorts since the 1990s, so we had to go to the centre to get me some from one of the Chinese markets. Once I had my shorts and flip-flops I was able to enjoy myself, although I was self-conscious with my skin so pale that I reflected as much sunlight as the moon.

Whereas Krasnoyarsk used to be known as a strategic military city, which was closed to Westerners, it is now known as the Russian City of Fountains. This is due to the work of the previous mayor Pyotr Pimashkov, who restored all of the Soviet fountains after they fell into disrepair and threw in some new ones for good measure. It's impossible to walk or take a bus ride without passing at least one. Although people are not technically allowed to splash around in them, everyone seemed to be at it, so we did it too. It was so hot we spent whole days in the city centre walking from fountain to fountain, getting soaked to the skin and eating ice creams. When militia passed in their cars, Nastya cautioned me to stop jumping so hard in the fountains as they might pull over and have a word with me, but they never did. As long as you don't make a public nuisance of yourself, they leave you alone. My whole first week back in Krasnoyarsk was spent this way. It was bliss. I would even dare to call it paradise if it wasn't for the mosquitoes. Unfortunately, these little blood thirsty bastards stage an annual invasion of Russia every June and bugger off again in October. Night-time was the worst. It was so hot that we couldn't leave the window closed, but when it was open, hundreds of mozzies would stream in. We compromised by leaving the window open just a fraction and invested a hundred roubles in one of those plugin anti-mosquito devices that fills the air with scenty stuff and makes mosquitoes breakdance. However, the sound of mosquitoes buzzing away as the madness took them was just as annoying, and when I woke in the morning I had to shake their little corpses off the bed cover and out of my hair.

Ira

Nataliya Petrovna's mother was back from the hospital and living in the small back room next to Nastya's. Because of the language barrier, I never engaged in conversation with her, and neither did Nastya. Opportunities didn't present themselves as she spent most days in her room listening to the radio. Nastya's parents had gone to live at the dacha, though one of them would come back every day to give Ira her pills. Ira had a dodgy heart and needed looking after, having aged rapidly since a bad fall ten years earlier. Before this she had apparently been quite spritely. Nastya told me that after Ira's accident all those years ago, anyone who would lend a hand had to spend many hours a day coaxing Ira back onto her feet. She hadn't quite given up the will to live but had given up the will to walk. Thankfully everyone's efforts were successful.

In the middle of the afternoon Ira would make her daily trip to the balcony, to sit and watch the world go by. To get there, to get anywhere, Ira, hunched and frail, would lean on a small wooden stool and inch it forward. Every journey she made was equivalent to a long mountain trek for someone in the prime of their life. The sound of that stool scraping across the floor haunted me, especially at night. Ira – silent and solitary – was a kind of ghost. She existed and yet she wasn't present in our lives. When she was younger, she had been a highly celebrated Soviet scientist and engineer. Having studied at the Yekaterinburg polytechnic at PhD level, she went on to become a leading specialist in platinum and other rich metals. However, she never managed to finish her PhD as her tutor passed away, and there was nobody to replace him at the time. Ira went on to marry Pyotr Karbovski, and had three children, two of whom are now dead. When her husband passed away, it was felt that the best place for her was with her one surviving daughter.

Regardless of Ira's failing health, she still managed to maintain a normal dignified appearance. Before I woke in the morning, she would already be dressed in a long flowing gown and wore a red beret to mask her thinning hair. She made regular trips to the bathroom, sat on her stool and washed as best she could. She even cooked all her own meals and did the washing up if we left any dirty dishes by the sink. I was impressed by her stamina and will to continue living as normal a life as possible but sad that she spent so much time alone. To remedy the loneliness of senior citizens, Russian social services provide retired soviet comrades with state of the art mobile phones. Ira had one; I heard her talking on it quite often, though I don't think she knew what any of the other applications were for.

With my brother-in-law Dima and his wife, Marina, working every day, their son Semka would normally spend his weekday evenings with his grandparents. Although they were hardly at the apartment in summer, when they were, Semka would pretend to be afraid of Ira, and nicknamed her Baba Yaga. In Russia Baba Yaga is a fairy-tale witch that chases people around in her dacha, which has a pair of legs of its own. Ira, who we would normally refer to as Baba Ira, as Baba is short for grandmother in Russian, was called Baba Yaga so many times by Semka that I made the mistake of referring to her by that name also. Thankfully Nastya always managed to put her hand over my mouth at the right moment when her mother was around, as she would have been upset by it.

Superstitions

Some people believe in the strangest things. My mother believes her grandmother, my great Nana-Collie was a witch who could make people fall in love with others, or make people ill, by planting certain roots in the back garden with a bit of that person's hair. My mother still practises some of this stuff and reads tarot cards for my sisters and me once a year. Though I don't quite share my mother's views, I can forgive her mystic beliefs as they are, for the most part, quite unobtrusive. The same can't be said for Russian superstitions. For although they are charming in their own way, I have occasionally been really annoyed by either being told not to walk around something, or to say hello a hundred times in the street. It isn't simply a case of not walking under ladders or stepping on the cracks. Russian superstitions are extremely common and practised by almost every Siberian I know; if they are not carefully observed at all times it's possible to cause a great deal of offence. During my earlier visit I had witnessed occasional references to certain mystical beliefs, but it wasn't until summer that I fully understood the extent of them.

Nataliya Petrovna, who occasionally suffers from high blood pressure, would sometimes use very archaic methods to get this pressure down to an acceptable level. While we watched TV, she would sit with a jar of leeches bought earlier in the day, and attach two behind each ear. They were horrible to look at, and even worse when they were all fat with blood. They wriggled and writhed like the eels that were put into Commander Chekov's ear in the *Star Trek II: The Wrath of Khan*. When she had the leeches on the ear, I felt compelled to watch them grow bigger. With each passing minute they evolved from slithers into full grown monsters. It was during one of these evenings that Nataliya Petrovna, complete with 'eels' behind the ear, sat down with Nastya and me to discuss superstitions.

Before leaving for a long journey, travellers, and all those saying goodbye are supposed to sit for a moment in silence before the travellers depart. This allows time to sit and think of anything you may have forgotten but it's also supposed to bring you some luck. When I left Siberia at the end of spring, we had to begin our travels at 5.30 a.m. I hadn't slept and therefore was a bit irksome. I had taken the time to pack the night before and so after a shower and a cuppa I was ready on time. I have always made a point of being exactly on time in everything that I do. Nastya it seems is the exact opposite. She woke up late, insisted on breakfast, and took half an hour in the shower. Boris, whose job it was to take us to the airport, woke up even later. When I was really quite pissed off, and full of anxiety over the possibility of missing the flight, Nataliya Petrovna *insisted* on us sitting for a few minutes in silence. While this apparently brought a sense of calm to everyone else, it made me want to scream. But this is another major cultural difference. In Siberia, there is an attitude of 'We'll get there when we get there'. Nastya for example is always late for work. And if Boris says he'll take you somewhere at say 4:30 p.m., you always know you have time to see a movie before he is actually ready three hours later. It's not just my Siberian family. Nearly every Siberian I know is relaxed when it comes to schedules. I don't know whether it's a British thing, or a Welsh thing, or whether it's just me but I've worn the same watch on my wrist for twenty years as a means to be punctual and not upset people. It's hard for me to understand why other people don't do the same.

There are many more Siberian superstitions. Apparently it is forbidden to demonstrate something bad that happened to you or someone else in the past using your own or someone else's body. For instance, if you're talking about a broken arm you had as a kid or a time when you saw someone with a broken arm, you couldn't point towards your own arm and say 'it was like this', because, according to Siberian superstition, your own arm would soon become broken. If you do point to yourself without thinking while in the midst of conversation you then have to 'grab' the bad energy you just put into yourself and throw it into the air, then blow on your hands to clean them also. This one has brought me no end of irritation. When talking to Nastya, I often use hand gestures to emphasise certain words or point to a limb of mine when talking about previous accidents of others. No sooner have I pointed to the limb, I am always stopped mid-sentence and brushed down. Even if we are in the middle of the street Nastya will do this unashamedly, which was a little bit embarrassing for me at first but I got used to it after the hundredth time.

Returning home for forgotten things is especially bad. It rouses all kinds of demons and Slavic monsters from wherever they live. If you have forgotten something it's considered wise to leave it behind, but if you absolutely have to go back and get it you should look in the mirror with your tongue hanging out before leaving again. There were times when I left my gloves at home by mistake in the spring, which left me no choice but to go back for them. When I did, Nastya pleaded with me to poke my tongue out in front of the mirror and wiggle it about for a second. This was horrendously funny to me, but to Nastya it was a very serious issue. I couldn't help laughing, and when faced with Nastya's scornful expression it just made it all the funnier.

If a bird lands outside your window you have to tap the glass to get it to bugger off. Although if a bird accidentally flies into the glass or taps on it, beware, because this will rouse the Slavic bird monsters. If a bird flies through an open window and spends some time inside, this is considered the worst of all. This means someone in your family will die soon or accidentally be squashed by evils. This one was already familiar to me as my mother used to say 'If you see a white owl on the windowsill you will die'. As a young boy, I took this quite seriously and as a test I spent a number of hours at the window to see if I could spot one. I never did though. There aren't many white owls in Cardiff apparently.

People walking down the street together must never walk on opposite sides of any given obstacle; they must choose one side or the other, even if they end up walking in single file. Again, while walking with Nastya, she often pulled me around bollards or other people as a means to keep us together. Observing this ritual makes it almost impossible to get somewhere in a hurry. If we did end up walking around something separately, she insisted on us saying 'Hello' to each other. We're supposed to say it a hundred times, but I tend to stop after two.

Birthday parties must never be celebrated before the actual date. If you wish someone a happy birthday before the day, they might suffer some sort of bad luck or devils will come. Talking about future success, whistling in the apartment, putting an empty bottle back on the table, shaking hands across the threshold of a doorway, and not draining your glass before you put it down, all bring bad luck or raise devils. I'm sorry to say that I have been guilty of all of these at some point or another and with so many superstition rules broken it is likely that I've raised enough devils to cause quite a commotion. So if I have inadvertently instigated some sort of future apocalypse, I apologise. The only Siberian rule that I do observe and quite agree with is that if you have alcohol, it must be drunk until it's gone.

Water is also a big deal in Russia. I suffer from psoriasis, one of the ugliest of skin diseases. This autoimmune disorder is incurable, although cortisones and creams with a high steroid content can keep it at bay. During the winter of 2010, my psoriasis erupted, and turned from a small patch of blisters on my chest to a patch of red that covered 90 per cent of me. With my skin peeling from my face, I looked more like a burns victim. In fact, many of my friends asked if I had been in a fire. Before the arrival of summer in 2011, I had managed to soften most of the effects using steroid creams, although this is only a short-term fix. The closest thing to a cure is a high dosage of – or a prolonged exposure to – UV rays.

In February 2011, I was referred to a specialist in the NHS who recommended I volunteer myself for what is known as 'light therapy'. This involves being zapped by a shockingly powerful sunbed several times a week over a three-month period. Light therapy is an extreme measure and so one is only allowed a relatively low number of five-minute exposures in a lifetime. Having had psoriasis since I was twenty-three, and knowing that the sun is one giant source of UV, I decided to opt out of my hospital treatment and go sunbathing instead. Controlled and regulated sunbathing is a method I had used before in the UK, only with my condition so bad I needed a warmer climate. This is why I chose to spend as much of July as I could sunbathing at the dacha. Nastya however didn't believe any of this, and thought the only possible way for me to be cured would be a trip to some 'magic lake' with healing minerals. Either this or rubbing my skin with some kind of oily cloth; the oil would be magic of course. While rubbing oil or moisturiser into dry psoriasis skin can rejuvenate it for a day, it is no cure. As a compromise, I alternated sunbathing on the lawn outside the dacha with swimming in a lake close by. The sun did its job and burned off the majority of my psoriasis skin, leaving me slightly pink and a little tanned. Although Nastya saw the effects of my methods, she still insisted on knowing better. Having had my disease for many years, and having tried every possible cure going, from NHS-recommended creams to the very ridiculous series of magnets worn on the wrist, there was nobody who knew how to deal with psoriasis better than me. Being told everything I knew was somehow wrong and that I could be 'cured' by magic was rather hurtful.

In some parts of Russia there is still a belief that natural cures are more powerful than modern medicine. I know that most modern pain relievers and anaesthetics are synthetic versions of real herbs designed to emulate the effect of natural healing qualities found in plants. I can't argue against those who believe in natural remedies – I was, after all, temporarily healed by the sun – however, I think that relying purely on alternative medicine can be detrimental to one's health. For instance, early in July Nastya was taken to hospital suffering abdominal pain, and was informed that she had a small kidney stone that needed to be operated on. Instead of accepting this and having the small operation required, Nastya, who is highly influenced by Boris, decided to take her problem to a Chinese herbalist who prescribed all sorts of fluids and pills created from natural herbs. Regardless of continued discomfort, she was adamant that the herbs she had ingested would work over a long period of time, when in fact we had no proof that they were doing anything at all.

Several years before, while out looking for deer, Boris was bitten by a Siberian grass tick and consequently spent a month in hospital. Since his release, Boris has suffered from occasional erratic behaviour, and mood swings, which are all attributed to tick-borne encephalitis. As a result he became quite paranoid with regard to his and everyone else's health. As well as seeing a trained doctor, Boris also visits a Chinese herbalist at least once a month and each time he returns he is convinced that he has a new family of worms inside him. Nastya and I both agree that the damage caused by the bug bite is allowing him to be exploited, and yet she herself refused to see a trained medical professional with her kidney stone.

Nastya is so highly influenced by what I refer to as 'mumbo jumbo' it occasionally puts a strain on our relationship. While out walking somewhere, Nastya is convinced that we pick up 'microbes' (pronounced meek-robes). These microbes are apparently evil and stick to your shoes and your trousers when you're out and about. When I came home, if I wore the same trousers while sitting down on a chair or the bed, Nastya would shout 'Now you have infected that with meekrobes.' I don't see the logic in it. If I take off my jeans and hang them on the back of the chair, the chair is then infected, which will infect the floor, anything that walks on the floor, and eventually the bed. There was a similar instance in Paris where Nastya said she couldn't sit on the stone wall next to the Seine with me because 'If a woman sits on stone she gets ill in her ladyparts.' I'm not sure if that is true or not, but there were several other couples sat on that stone wall in Paris that seemed to be just fine. Though Nastya loves romance, her weird and wonderful belief system can often kill the moment.

Domovoi

Another thing we should have probably discussed before getting married was Nastya's belief in little men, or little, invisible, bearded men to be more precise. The domovoi is a small man who Nastya and many other Russians believe lives in one's apartment or dacha. Although it is said to be a house spirit of sorts, Nastya, among others, claims to have 'seen him.'

Apparently domovoi are always male, about a foot tall, have long beards or are totally covered in hair, like Dougal from *The Magic Roundabout*; though I prefer to think of domovoi as being like the goblins from Jim Henson's film *Labyrinth*. Partly because I love David Bowie, and if domovoi are real, I'd like them to be like Hoggle, the dwarf who led Sarah into the labyrinth; even though Sarah was a girl, when I was young I very much wanted to be in her shoes so I could get to see David Bowie dance his *Magic Dance*.

Traditionally, every home is said to have its domovoi, although according to Nastya, domovoi only live in good houses or apartments. To quote Nastya directly: 'He turns off taps if you leave them on when you go out, and if he doesn't turn off the tap he will do something by magic which makes you remember, like send you a cosmic mental signal. Many relatives have seen him. He is white, very hairy, and has a long nose.'

Domovoi are often held responsible for items in the home being mislaid or lost. Some believe he simply likes to play tricks on people, while others believe that he is angered by messiness and/or foul language. This would explain why only Nastya's things go missing. She often leaves unwashed dishes in the bedroom and has a habit of carpeting the floor every morning with clothes from the wardrobe. Nastya also has a terrible habit of losing earrings. With the exception of a pair we bought in Paris, she seems incapable of owning a complete pair for more than a day. Usually after looking for the missing earring for five minutes, Nastya would blame its absence on domovoi. If you suspect that your stuff has been stolen by domovoi it is said that if you ask for it back aloud, he will magically return what you've been looking for, usually in a place you've already looked. According to Nastya, it helps if you leave out a bowl of something sweet. Nastya very much believes in this. In fact, many Siberians I've spoken to believe that domovoi are as real as the words you see before you. Some say he likes to do the washing up when everyone is asleep, while others say he lives behind the oven or at the back of the wardrobe, and comes out at night to see you've swept the floor properly. One person even told me that they had woken one night to find a domovoi sat on their chest and no matter how hard they tried, they couldn't lift their arms to push him away. I've actually heard other stories similar to that one, which is disturbing. If I woke to find some malevolent bearded goblin sat on my chest, and I had lost all strength in my arms, I'd probably leave Russia at the first available opportunity.

While this all sounds like complete and utter madness, you must remember that to many Russians the domovoi are part of real life. Though some laugh at the idea of house spirits, my mother-in-law being one of them, they still attribute the safe return of some item (that may have been lost) to a supernatural power; if not domovoi, then something equally magic. After all, missing keys don't return themselves. While I am not entirely convinced by the existence of domovoi, my love for Jim Henson films and the fact I went to see *The Lord of the Rings: the Fellowship of the Ring* in the cinema six times (seven if you count *The Lord of the Rings* cinema marathon in 2003) makes it an easier superstition to accept, and even enjoy. There is sweetness to it, and though it may be totally bonkers to believe in little men who live in the wardrobe and who love to wash the dishes, people have believed in way more far-fetched ideas. For instance, some people believe a bearded man in the sky decided to make the earth in seven days, apparently for no good reason at all. Perhaps when he was casting humans in his big holy Plaster of Paris moulds, he made a few domovoi as practice runs. Who knows?

Aeroflot Flight SU247. August 17th 2011. Moscow — London

Just as she had in the spring, Nastya accompanied me to Moscow. This was unnecessary as I had a connecting flight to London in the evening but again we didn't know when I would next return to Russia. We arrived in Moscow at around 11 a.m., leaving us only seven hours before I had to be back at the airport. It was horrendously hot, so instead of running around the city trying to see the touristy things we had missed previously we headed straight for one of Moscow's parks. Moscow is actually one of the greenest capitals in the world with over a hundred parks to choose from. We chose Kolomenskoye Park, which is full of old white church buildings and ancient archways. It used to be royal estate and covers a 390-hectare area that overlooks the steep banks of the Moskva River.

Near one of the modern outdoor restaurants was a temperature gauge, which read 44°C. Who would have thought Moscow could be so bloody hot? As we had taken a night flight and were a little overdressed, we spent five hours lying in the park, and skimming stones across the river. The weather was as good as it could have been and we lamented not having more time. When we had to leave, Nastya decided we should take a walk around Red Square and the complete Kremlin Wall. There were thousands of people eating ice-lollies and drinking water from plastic bottles; just in front of the Iberian Chapel, in the short passage connecting Red Square with Manezhnaya Square is Moscow's Zero point plaque. All distances from Moscow's centre are measured from this point. It is said that if you make a wish and throw a coin over your shoulder onto the plaque, it will come true. Many people were testing this theory. Next to a circle of people throwing coins over their shoulders were two babushkas. They picked up every coin no sooner than it hit the ground. This was too much for one little boy, who after throwing his coin onto the plaque, immediately bent down, picked it up and threw it into the distance. I thought his action was a little mean but at the same time, I could understand it. With someone picking up the coins, and even bending down in readiness before you've even tossed it, the small moment of magic you're paying for is quite lost.

After more tearful farewells and many hugs in Sheremetyevo, I was once again alone on a plane full of Russians. We still had no plans, hardly any money, and yet for some reason we thought it would all magically work out for the good. This was actually Nastya's philosophy. She often said things like 'It will all work out; you think too much'. Perhaps I did. After Paris I wasn't sure if we would see each other again. There were such long periods between meetings that I did lose faith a number of times. But as we were married and I was leaving Russia for the second time, I began to worry less about the future and employed Nastya's way of thinking.

London's Burning

About a week before I left Russia for the second time, two memorable things happened that are worthy of mention. The first being that Nastya bought us a toaster. This may sound insignificant but it was a huge life-changing moment for me. Nastya's family had no concept of a full English breakfast, and toast was something that people ate in the mythical land of Wales while riding dragons. We had eaten meatballs or soup for breakfast most mornings and I was a little tired of it. So you can imagine how happy I was when Nastya presented me with a toaster, sliced bread and a jar of Nutella. The second thing that happened was the summer riots in England, which became a major news item in Russia.

I had been lying happily on the bed when Nastya bust into our bedroom and said 'There is war in London.'

'With who?'

'With London.'

I got up and went to the living room to see for myself on the TV. Though I couldn't understand what was being said I could see scenes of rioting and understood what Nastya had meant. I wasn't surprised by the riots. After the MPs' expenses scandal of 2009, it had seemed to me as though the air in Britain had been charged with anger for some while. Nastya saw this as an excuse to keep me in Russia. She said 'You could apply to become a refugee.' But I knew that wouldn't be necessary, though I did allow myself to wonder for a second how nice it would have been to be given refugee status. Over the following days I followed the story online. Nastya was concerned the riots, which had spread out of London, would reach Wales. It never happened, and I sighed with relief because I love Cardiff. I'd seen it change over the years, and there were bad bits as well as good bits, but I couldn't stand the thought of people burning it down.

Unfortunately, the riots gave the impression that the British had become so infected by greed they would resolve to become criminals in order to get the latest flat screen TV or mobile phone. On the surface it did indeed look that way, and I was embarrassed for Britain. What made it worse was the view that the people looting were the same people who lived on benefits, and were used to getting things for free. Almost everyone I spoke to in Krasnoyarsk at that time seemed to think that the UK had become infected by greed, and it was very hard for me to get them to look at the situation from a different perspective. What they did not know was how those people looting lived in a world where there were few job opportunities, where they could be dependent on benefits for a long time when they did not want to be, all the while being demonised for the simple fact that they had nothing to lose.

I explained that people receiving benefits legally were actually normal everyday folk, and that the welfare state was a very good thing. When I was growing up my mum had two jobs and my dad always worked, however as my parents didn't make enough money for a bigger house they'd had to sleep on the living room floor for twenty years. And though they worked full time, they had still needed to claim child benefit; which I can say without exaggeration, was a lifesaver. Even then my mother had to miss meals, because she couldn't afford to feed her children *and* herself. At the age of twelve, I went to study at Glan Ely High School. At the time it had the world's worst reputation; apparently everyone who left there either became a dole-ite or ended up in prison. As I had done reasonably well in Junior School I was expected to leave High School with decent grades and leave all the other students behind. What happened was the opposite. Every person who I knocked about with during those years went on to do well, that is until the financial meltdown of 2007, yet Ely is often spoken of as the part of Cardiff where scroungers live. Perhaps there are a couple of people there who cheat the system, but when you listen to the news you'd think half the population were greedy benefits cheats. I find it difficult to feel hostility to people who cheat the system at the bottom of the food chain anyway, because I've seen first-hand what goes on at the top.

I actually worked in a British bank for five years and was witness to serious banking malpractice. I saw how customers who complained were treated better and given compensation if they had a savings account; how people with small incomes were recklessly loaned huge mortgages that they could barely afford; in my view the system that was supposed to prevent over-lending was actually designed to allow people into amounting huge debts that some would obviously default on. All this, and yet the man who ran the bank was at the same time the deputy chairman of the Financial Services Authority. The procedure for complaining about malpractice was that you were supposed to relay any grievances to your boss, who would then speak to their boss and so on. But how can you discuss such problems when the very man at the top of the company is also at the top of the investigating organisation? That's why the riots happened. Because millionaires who steal millions get a slap on the wrist while poor folk go to prison for much less. The riots *were* caused by greed, but greed at the top of the food chain, not the bottom as it was widely depicted. This of course was news to Nastya who until that time had viewed the UK as a place much less corrupt than Russia.

Aeroflot Flight SU781. December 19th 2011. Moscow — Krasnoyarsk

When I had arrived back in the UK in August, after taking the National Express to Cardiff, I found myself in Wood Street just after 1 a.m. on a Wednesday night. I thought the streets would be quiet, but they weren't. Cardiff was teaming with drunks. There were people smashing bottles, fighting, spitting, and the obligatory drunken women asleep by the side of the road. It was ironic that, coming from the former USSR, I hadn't felt any fear for a whole month until I returned to my home city. I had arranged to stay at my friend Peter's for the night because he lives on the Taff Embankment. With my laptop bag slung over my shoulders, I dragged my heavy suitcase across the Wood Street Bridge. It was a huge comedown after such a lovely day in Moscow.

Arriving at Peter's house, I was dismayed to find he was asleep and hadn't left the key under the flowerpot as arranged. I banged the door for 30 minutes, loud enough to wake him, but quiet enough not to wake the whole street. He didn't wake up. After a few panicked phone calls I was rescued by my friend Torben, who lives close to the little Tesco further up Lansdowne Road. Not only did he get up to make a spare bed up for me, but he also made me breakfast and coffee. I woke the next day at 4 p.m. Good old Torben had gone to work, leaving me to sleep off my travel weariness. Before I left, I made sure to leave a bar of Soviet chocolate in his living room as a thank you. A small price to pay for such reliable friendship.

Exactly like the previous time I returned to Britain, I was sad, lonely, and desperately clawing at whatever jobs I could find. By day I was either labouring, privately editing homework of literary students at Glamorgan University, doing poetry readings whenever they were offered, or working as a stage assistant in Chapter Arts Centre. By night I was either at my dad's house or my mum's but then Nastya would still phone me every day which, if I'm honest, made things worse. The separation was only bearable if I worked long hours and didn't think of my situation.

By November, we still had no plan for the future. There seemed nothing for it but to return to Krasnoyarsk. I applied for a Russian tourist visa in early November, the forty-five day rule still applied and so I couldn't book my flights until mid to late November. Fortunately I had worked so much since August that I had plenty of money. I had never been to Russia in the winter. It wasn't going to be like spring where I got away with wearing long socks, jeans and a jumper, and there was definitely no need to pack the shorts I had bought in summer. This time I needed serious gear. I spent the last week of November shopping online for arctic gloves, an elasticated neck wrap, thermals and plenty of cheap long-sleeved t-shirts. Proper winter jackets cost a fortune in the UK, and I didn't know for sure if they would be good enough for -30 °C. After much indecision I ended up not buying one.

This was going to be our first European Christmas together, so I had to busy myself with buying gifts. On my previous trip I had taken a variety of chocolates with me, including every kind of chocolate bar made by Cadbury, and one or two Terry's Chocolate Oranges. Nastya had fallen in love with the Chocolate Oranges, and because she hadn't had Wispa or Crunchie bars since Soviet times, she had begged me to bring more. When I left the UK, my suitcase was 19 kilos (1 kilo off my limit): 12 kilos of clothes; 7 kilos chocolate. It felt strange to be in possession of so many Chocolate Oranges. When I was a kid, my dad had used the salad container in the fridge as his own personal storage space for all things forbidden to children. Being a curious little boy, I had a peek in there from time to time. It was always filled with Chocolate Oranges. Because of this I associated them with my dad and avoided them when I got older, because they were 'for adults'. It had been drummed into me from a very young age that my parents liked to have their own sweet things, which were somehow superior to the chocolates we ate as kids. With a bag full of forbidden adult candy I felt like I was stealing from my father in some way, and exporting to Russia something that was rightfully his.

The journey couldn't have gone smoother. I arrived at Heathrow on time, even though I had stayed up getting blotto with Torben the night before. In the past I had been able to stay at Peter's house for a few hours, before waking up and walking for a few short minutes to Wood Street where the buses left from. This wasn't possible any more as Peter had some work issues and couldn't afford to be disturbed or receive guests. I needed a new accomplice. Someone who lived near the station and who wouldn't mind me crashing at their place from 10 p.m. to 4 a.m. I didn't have to wait long before I was rescued once again by Torben, who not only didn't mind helping me but seemed to enjoy it. The only major difference was that when I stayed at Torben's, he insisted on us getting totally rat-arsed while singing songs badly until I had to leave.

From Heathrow I flew to Moscow, waited until late evening, caught my connecting flight, and was passing over the Ural Mountains just as the sun was coming up. The morning began with sun beams striking the tops of the Urals while eating chicken, roast potatoes and gravy with the obligatory small slice of bread. It was one of life's perfect moments. Though Siberia is famous for being one of the coldest places on Earth, it was hard for me to conceive the reality of what I was heading for, having only experienced Russia in spring and summer. I couldn't wait to see Nastya again, and I was excited to see how happy my bag of oranges would make her; however I wasn't really looking forward to being holed up in the apartment for another month. In summer we had had the option of sleeping at the dacha, which broke up the monotony of being stuck in the apartment so long.

Summer at the Dacha

In August the dacha had been a totally different place to what I had glimpsed at Easter. For a start, there was a lot more greenery, and in place of the last snowfalls of spring there were lots of flowers, butterflies and various foodstuffs growing in the garden. Like many dacha owners, Nastya's parents prefer to grow their own vegetables when they've got the chance. When Boris isn't out in the taiga, the dacha is his favourite place in the entire world. As well as vegetables and fruits, he also spends a lot of time cultivating patches of herbs from which he makes energy drinks and medicines. He seemed to have a great knowledge of the properties of each plant. Some of which he taught himself, but many things would have been handed down from his parents.

Food preparation is the same at the dacha but as there is a lack of running water, it's not so easy to wash the dishes well. Sometimes I watched in horror as chopping boards used to cut meat were simply rinsed with a bit of cold water and put away again. I often got a bad stomach. When I was ill, Boris gave me little vials of medicine to drink; but if I was really ill he would give me some bark to chew on from some tree at the end of the garden. I can't say whether I was actually cured by this or if I was simply distracted by the acrid taste in my mouth.

When Nataliya Petrovna wasn't chopping meats or watering the crops in the garden, she spent a lot of time pickling things in jars. Siberians are very fond of the mushrooms that grow wild and locally but much prefer them pickled, as they do their cabbage. The balcony at the apartment was often full of jars of pickled things that would then be saved for winter. I often felt, as I watched Nataliya Petrovna pick through buckets of mushrooms and drop them into their relative jars, that I was alive inside Gogol's story of Afanasy Ivanovich and Pulkheria Ivanovna. Had Nataliya Petrovna had a cat, and had it gone missing, I am sure she would have interpreted this as some sort of mystic sign like the one Pulkheria Ivanovna did in Gogol's story. When they were bickering, as they often did, they also reminded me of Urgl and Engywook from *The Neverending Story*, with Boris as Engywook looking up from his mixed herbs on the table, with eyes magnified through his goggles, exclaiming he had invented some kind of new fantastical remedy.

Many times during that period, Nataliya Petrovna would ask me to fetch her something or other from the garden so we could have it for supper. It was strange for me, having to take a knife and cut free a few tomatoes, or dig up a few potatoes, because I had come from a world where everything we ate was bought in a supermarket. When I wanted to drink tea, Nastya would say 'Well go to the garden and get some then'. This sometimes left me confused. Although I understood what I needed to do, the instruction, though logical, was so alien to me that I became rooted to the spot.

With no plumbing at the dacha, more primitive methods are employed to wash, and clean teeth. At the end of each day, the bucket of slops from under the sink would be full of water, vegetable peelings, and soap bubbles. This then has to be taken to the end of the garden, and poured into a home-made trough full of soil and worms. As I wasn't much use when it came to growing things it became my responsibility to make sure this was done.

Visiting the toilet is also something that needs to be done outside. Most dachas have a small outhouse at the end of the garden – a wooden seat, on a wooden plinth, with basic shelter. All the offerings to nature fall through the hole in the seat, into a specially dug chamber in the ground. This pit of poops can be a bit pongy in the summer and attracts more than a few flies, which in turn attract spiders. I tried avoiding this place at first, which was of course impossible.

To get water, someone has either to fill up bottles at the apartment and drive them to the dacha, or go to the fresh water generator near the local lake. Though our dacha had a large square tank filled with lake water, we obviously couldn't drink it. Without many responsibilities, I often volunteered to fetch the water from the generator using a little wooden cart with bicycle wheels Boris had made specially. To get there I had to drag this contraption along dacha roads, which are so full of potholes that it caused my cart to lean precariously, sometimes next to parked cars. Another obstacle: the pipes on the roads. These pipes were the very ones that carried lake water to our steel box in the garden. Whoever laid them hadn't bothered with attempting to bury them, which meant they were driven over by cars and carts every day.

At the generator, to get the water out I had to place my plastic containers beneath a makeshift hose, and then plug the generator into an outside electric socket built into a concrete wall. It always began by making a horrible whirring sound, before water came gushing out. This water is free and anyone can have as much as they can carry. In some districts, where there is no fresh water generator, they have old-fashioned hand pumps that are plumbed into natural sources of water underground. These are not as common and much less convenient as not only do you have to physically exert yourself to get the water out, but the water can run dry in summer. Our generator also stopped sometimes. It's not that it broke, it was simply that there was no fresh water available. This kind of thing had happened a few times at the apartment; the water would be switched off without reason or warning. This could be very annoying if you were in the shower, covered in bubbles. It was even more annoying if you were in the middle of the shower and only the cold or hot water was switched off, leaving you burnt or frozen on the spot. Sometimes this lack of water at the apartment could last for several days. I am not sure why it happened and nobody else seemed to know either. I put it down to a need for regular maintenance as the result of pipes bursting in winter, or pipes being laid without much thought as they were throughout the dacha territories.

There are two ways of washing at the dacha. Russians are very fond of sitting in a sauna or *banya*. Although Dima has one built apart from his dacha, during the summer of 2011 I was too afraid to use it. In Boris's dacha there is an indoor washing area that can also be used as a sauna. It never is though, as Nataliya Petrovna is worried the constant steam will warp the wood or make it soft. Instead, to get clean, Boris set up some steel poles in the garden with a shower curtain wrapped round them. This is where I washed. I would take two buckets of cold water and pour them over me, one pre-soap, one to rinse; because it was so hot, there was no need to heat any water. This method has a real lack of privacy to it. Although it was strange at first, I eventually got used to seeing more of people's flesh than I normally would; either someone is walking semi-naked from the banya to the dacha, or Boris is digging in a small pair of shorts, or Nastya and Marina are sunbathing in the garden with nearly everything on show. I was at first very self-conscious of my body, because it is pale and I have psoriasis, but it was too hot to really care too much about this, and I really needed to heal my skin.

When going to sleep in the dacha there was a similar lack of privacy that I had to get accustomed to. Nastya and I slept in a double bed, behind the stove in the original section of the dacha; and because the stove and chimney don't make a complete wall, a curtain was strung up as a divider. At night I could not only hear the grunts and snoring of Boris, whose favourite bed was the single one on the other side of the curtain, but I suspected that he could hear Nastya and I if we had some boinka-boinka. I was a little weirded-out by this, but Boris either politely ignored it, or was too fast asleep to notice. At the dacha during the night, it's possible to hear what people would normally get up to behind closed doors, but it's okay; like anywhere people engage in natural things, they have their bodies on show when it's sunny, and occasionally have sex at night. This isn't to say that people regularly take their kit off in front of everyone and get busy on the lawn. On the contrary, Nastya's parents seemed quite prudish. If they did the boinka-boinka, we never heard them, and Nastya was always worried about them hearing us.

The most popular food in Russia throughout summer is *shashliks*, otherwise known as shish kebab. Russians love *shashliks* and spend a lot of time preparing them. The meat is usually marinated overnight in vinegar, or wine, with a range of herbs and spices, before being arranged on skewers. These are roasted on a trough or barbeque and are the highlight of Russian dacha time. To cook them, we had to first let Semka build the fire. He insisted on bringing the wood and making the fire himself. He would have cooked the *shashliks* too if it weren't for the fact the barbeque trough was taller than he was.

Across from Boris's dacha is another belonging to Dima and Marina and next to this is Marina's flower patch: a small circle of flora and fauna with sunflowers at the centre. The sunflowers aren't merely for show. Every member of my Siberian family loves nothing more than to sit for hours eating sunflower seeds. After putting whole shells in their mouths, they have the ability to crunch out the seed, swallow it, and then spit out the bits of shell into a cup. No matter how many times I tried, I couldn't master this without eating the shells.

A small veranda at the front of Dima's dacha acted as the usual meeting place for everyone during summer. We often ate *shashliks* there. This was a pain at times, because both Nastya and her mother didn't really see eye-to-eye with Marina, and Marina didn't much like them either. But the trough for cooking *shashliks* had been permanently located at the front of Dima's dacha, so if we wanted to cook, we had no other choice but to go there. Though everyone tried to get along for the sake of Dima, who is a very calm and sober fellow, there were occasional heated exchanges between Nastya and Marina. These were normally preceded by two things. Either Marina had had a drop too much, which she was fond of doing at the weekend, or we had overstayed our welcome on their veranda. The smallest thing could lead to the most ferocious verbal battle, so I began spending less time at Dima's just to keep the peace.

At the end of July, Boris celebrated his sixty-third birthday. Although he doesn't drink or smoke, he didn't hold back from enjoying himself, albeit with fruit juices instead of alcohol. Besides the immediate family, Boris had invited a few guests – all regular folk except for one, a mathematician who had the same face and voice as Leonard Nimoy from the original *Star Trek* series. Although I wasn't able to communicate much with him, I spent a little too much time looking at his face, because it's not often you find yourself in the middle of Siberia drinking vodka with Spock.

Marina who had brought five bottles of Cognac, and who normally wouldn't attempt to speak English, plucked up the courage to say 'Michael, Cognac?' to which I would reply in my very awkward and basic Russian, 'Da' (yes). This led to my drinking at least one whole bottle of Cognac, and was likely the cause of my throwing up at 4 a.m. Nataliya Petrovna was a little disappointed by this as earlier in the evening she had said 'We have had English here before. They were sick.'

A Brit in Eastern Siberia is a bit of a novelty, though not completely unheard of thanks to the tourists who take the Trans-

Siberian throughout the year, but a Welshman is considered stranger company than someone from outer space. Nastya had to constantly explain to our guests that Wales is the little country that England is stuck to. Everyone was curious to learn how Nastya and I were planning to make a future for ourselves and when we would settle. Boris's guests somehow had the impression that everyone in the UK knows each other well because it is such a small place compared with the vastness of Russia. When Nastya's attention was diverted our guests still spoke to me, and I was lucky if I could understand just one per cent of the conversation. However there were a few words I did recognise, as they were spoken in English. Thankfully, due to a popular joke on television which pokes fun at professional Russian to English translators, a few Siberians are able to say Anthony Hopkins, Chicken McNuggets, Windows XP, together because (as a stock phrase), Britney Spears and Status Quo. Everyone was pleasantly surprised to learn Anthony Hopkins is in fact a Welshman, but slightly disappointed to learn that I didn't know him personally.

Like most events in Siberia that involve copious amounts of alcohol, the evening eventually descended into the inevitable wailings of karaoke. Unfortunately, the art of singing badly into a microphone is very popular all over Russia and there are a huge number of popular Russian tunes, none of which I knew how to sing. Fortunately for me there are a few old bands from the West that are still massive in Russia. After several Cognacs, I found myself singing Status Quo's 'In The Army Now' as a duet with Dima, followed by a double bill of Boney M – 'Rasputin' and 'Daddy Cool'. All bands groups and singers who have ever acknowledged Russia in a song have become favourites in Russia. This is also true for actors, such as Jude Law who played Vasily Zaytsev in *Enemy at the Gates* (2001), and Scarlett Johansson who played Natasha Romanoff in *Iron Man 2*. One of my first memories of Moscow is Jude Law's face printed on the giant advertisements for vodka hanging in Sheremetyevo Airport. Scarlett Johansson can often be seen on billboards advertising Russian saunas, though I'm not clear if these are authorised advertisements or not. When I first visited Russia in the spring, I vividly remember arriving in Krasnoyarsk on the Trans-Siberian. Through one of the windows, I saw a dacha where the roof had been made from a large recycled billboard and on this billboard was a huge cameo of Scarlett Johansson, partially covered in snow.

Just as I was falling asleep to the image of a snow-covered Scarlett Johansson, the pilot announced our descent. I'm not sure why, but every time I fly I always take a seat above the left wing of the plane. I think it has something to do with *The Twilight Zone*, which had a huge effect on me as a boy, and gave me nightmares for years after. If there is ever a gremlin on a wing, I need to be able to see it. Fortunately there were no gremlins and the flight was peaceful. When it came to landing, however, things changed rapidly. There was a very high wind and heavy snow fall. We glided over the city, over the forest and over the airport perimeter fence. Wheels were about to touch the ground. At the crucial moment a huge gust of wind took us off course, the plane lost balance, tipped to the left, and the left wing came horribly close to the tarmac. I thought we were fucked. Totally and utterly fucked. Thankfully Russian pilots are used to this kind of thing. After all, they take off and land in the world's worst flying conditions every day. At the point we were about to become pancakes, the engines roared and we flew high and left. The pilot then said something over the tannoy in Russian that I think was 'Hold onto your balls I'm going to try again'. The second time we came in fast and straight, and the pilot made use of the entire length of the runway. Russians have a tradition of clapping when a plane lands, and until that moment I had never understood it.

When everyone erupted into applause I couldn't help but join in. It was the first time I had ever participated in 'the clapping' and the first time I had almost become a pancake.

PART III

Aeroflot Flight SU241. January 16th 2011. Moscow — London

Following an all too brief first Christmas holiday in Krasnoyarsk, Nastya had flown to Moscow with me again in the early hours of the morning. We got to Yemelyanovo airport in good time and the subsequent flight to Moscow was uneventful. In Sheremetyevo airport, Nastya was as tearful as ever and wouldn't let me go even as I entered the booth where I had to surrender my immigration card. People are supposed to enter this booth alone to hand over their passport and papers, and the customs official usually holds up your passport against the glass in his little hut and compares your picture with your face, even though you're leaving the country. I guess this is to make sure nobody is leaving Russia pretending to be you. This time the customs man just smiled and looked away as Nastya and I kissed over and over again. When she finally let go of me the man scanned my passport, took the immigration card away and let me into the waiting room for international transfers.

Looking down over Moscow, sweltering in my snow boots and a large black hunting jacket, I couldn't help feeling I was a little overdressed for London. One of the immigration officials in Moscow had laughed after Nastya had left. He looked at me, then my passport, then back at me, and said 'You cold yes?' before laughing to himself. It seemed I was overdressed even by Moscow standards; God only knew what I would look like touching down in Heathrow. With yet another four hours to wait until I got there, I relaxed in my chair as much as I could with too many clothes on and thought of my Siberian winter adventure; happy that we finally had a plan, and confident I would take care of my end of things.

Winter in Russia

Nastya had picked me up from the airport in a taxi upon arrival from the UK in December; Boris was already on a hunting trip and Dima was having his well-earned Sunday lie-in. The drive from Yemelyanovo airport to Krasnoyarsk was bleak. The sky was dark grey and heavy with snow. There were huge banks of the white stuff either side of the motorway and the only parts of the road visible were track lines where previous cars had been. Still, it was busy. Our taxi driver weaved through the traffic at a hair-raising speed, completely ignoring the treacherous weather conditions. It was a sharp contrast to what I had experienced in the UK where the slightest sign of snow meant traffic crawling along at a snail's pace, and all the airports and trains coming to a halt. I was a bit frightened and made sure to fasten my seatbelt.

Russian roads can be a bit crazy. They drive on the right and are supposed to overtake on the left. What actually happens is they drive on anything that is flat, and overtake on anything including the hard shoulder; this creates semi-organised chaos. While driving at the speed of sound, our taxi very nearly got boxed in a few times by people also driving at the speed of sound. Fortunately, our taxi was a very shiny and expensive-looking Mercedes, and the driver was obviously aware of his capabilities. At the point I was sure we would be squished he put his foot down and increased acceleration to the speed of light. We flew down the motorway, and all the while trance tunes were playing on the radio with the driver bobbing his head to the beat while smoking a cigarette. He was quite a cool guy.

At the apartment we turned on the TV to pass the time and fill the air with noise. There was a breaking news item about Krasnoyarsk's Cheremshanka Airport, the sister airport just two miles west of Yemelyanovo. Even though it was snowing like billy-o, the terminal building and control tower had burned down during a mysterious four-hour blaze that took thirty-eight fire engines to extinguish. It seemed the fates had conspired to remind me that I had no travel insurance. Still, it was a few days before I went online and actually bought some.

That same day, after only a few hours' rest, we left for the city centre to see the Christmas decorations. The central avenue, Prospekt Mira, was fantastically decorated with lights in the trees, lights between all the buildings, and lights running up the street lamps. Every fountain had also been switched off because all the water had been replaced with light displays. I felt like I was alive inside a Christmas card, one of those pop-up cards that also play music. It may sound garish, but it didn't look or feel that way at all. It was a very different experience from the Christmas feeling I had known in Wales, and it was easy to become excited by it. There were no shoppers running around like headless chickens, instead I saw couples arm-in-arm – sometimes with a child wrapped up in fur – stopping to admire carousels in toyshop windows.

The central square located between Ulitsa Bograda and Ulitsa Dubrovinskogo becomes the gathering point for locals and tourists alike. This is because Krasnoyarsk has the largest Christmas tree in all of Russia, which stands at 46 metres. Surrounding this tree are dozens of intricate ice sculptures, ranging from 6 to 12 feet in height. There are many obvious subjects for the statues such as frozen people dancing, ice ships and wolves balancing balls on their noses but they also carve a few things you wouldn't expect such as giant sewing machines, penny farthings and ice telescopes. To keep the children amused they even make playgrounds – fortresses, labyrinths, and palaces – complete with staircases and slides that both children and adults play on. Beneath the Christmas tree was a large painting of

Grandfather Frost, the Russian equivalent of Father Christmas. He is the same as Father Christmas in most ways except that he apparently brings children presents in person, instead of when they are sleeping. As well as a long white beard, big black boots and a long red coat, he is often depicted as carrying a magical staff and is always accompanied by his granddaughter, Snegurochka, dressed in long silver-blue robes and a furry shapka.

The Russian winter attire is exactly as you would imagine. Thick coats and warm snow boots, though many people who work in offices wear fur-lined smart black shoes and woollen office coats over smart suits. Russian women, for the most part, wear full-length coats of various shapes and materials, and only those with large incomes, or rich husbands, wear black mink. I saw many of these wealthier women floating around with mink hoods obscuring their faces from view. There are an unusual number of tall women in Russia, and when they have their mink coats and high-heeled boots on, they look like goddesses, similar to the smartly dressed women I have seen floating about in Paris. The majority of these women are, as my mates would say, 'smokin' hot' with high cheekbones and perfectly-sculpted eyebrows. The men are less attractive – they are either tall and skinny or short and stocky. Men's haircuts are also less appealing, they often have very short fringes and mullet style locks at the back of short-cropped hair. Nastya and I would often comment when we saw a Siberian goddess float by with a small Russian man on her arm. It just didn't seem right. I think this is because old-fashioned gender roles are still common in Russia. Women are expected to look flawless, while men are expected to be very hard and very strong, which they are.

Being a Welshman I'm not afraid of much, but I do have a small list of things I wouldn't like to meet down a dark alley; Siberian men are on that list, along with Charles Bronson, and the scary robot-lady from *Superman 3*. Not only do Siberian men have a harder life, what with the weather and the dacha lifestyle, but the majority of them have to do compulsory military service before the age of twenty seven. By the time they are thirty they are tough as bears. The only reasons a man is exempt from military service are having two or more children, having a medical certificate declaring them unfit, or studying at university. All full-time students are free from conscription, but they can be drafted for one year after graduation. Those who continue full-time postgraduate education are not drafted. This, I suspect, is why Russia produces an inordinate number of great scientists and why their technology, especially their military technology is scarily advanced.

Although I had brought my own fake-fur ushanka from the UK, and I had a large woollen cardigan under my coat, it was insufficient to keep out the driving wind. My shapka let out too much heat and my coat, which was heavy and weather proof by British standards, felt thin as paper. Boris, who has a wardrobe full of spare hunting clothes lent me an old black winter coat that was two sizes too big for me, but very warm, and a real black mink ushanka. Because my British shapka was so thin, Boris asked me to give it to him. When he was climbing mountains in the taiga, while fighting off bears and stalking deer, his head would sweat too much under real fur, so a poorly-made British ushanka was perfect. With my huge black coat, black furry shapka and black snow boots I looked the part, and as I was now disguised as a Russian, Nastya and I were free to enjoy walks throughout the city and along the banks of the Yenisei without me freezing to death. One of the winter pleasures we often indulged in was buying *shashliks* from street stalls near the giant Christmas tree. From the middle of December to the first week of January a fleet of street merchants stand around the tree with mobile barbeques, selling a range of chicken, pork and beef *shashliks* on skewers. Despite the snow, the meat is always well cooked and very hot, although a bit pricey at times. Still I didn't mind paying over-the-odds for hot food, because it is so much better than anything available at the cafés.

Like the UK, Russia has a variety of cafés that differ in style and standard. The worst of them, which are mostly chains, offer lukewarm food that is often dry and boring. Instead of getting a full meal on one plate, like you can in any British café, you have to order things separately, which are then served on plastic disposable plates. There is normally a queue system in these cafés. They are designed so that you pick up a tray as you enter, collecting little dishes from counters as you shuffle along towards the till point. When you reach the till, the already lukewarm food is cold as British seawater. Known as stolovaya, this type of café was created during Soviet times and based on the school dinners system. Some of the other cafés are different in that they don't have a tray system and you only get your food when you pay for it at the counter or it is brought by a waiter. I preferred these places as they were the closest I could get to proper independent British cafés that serve proper hot grubbage, plus they were usually well decorated with wooden beams and soft lighting. I didn't often get to see them, however, as Nastya preferred to visit the cheapy-cheapy stolovaya she had grown up with. Although some of them were a modern take on the Soviet style, they were all quite similar in that they housed very tired and uncomfortable furniture. There is always a noticeable difference in clientele also. While the better cafés were usually full with people who knew how to smile, the stolovaya were crammed with the joyless faces, people who looked lost in thought and who I assumed weren't able to bring themselves to break free from Soviet discomfort.

While the older generations always wrapped up warm, younger folk occasionally didn't. I saw men wearing trainers, and women in their twenties wearing short skirts and thin pairs of tights. They must have been freezing. It seems wherever you go in the world there are always a few people who would rather sacrifice their health in order to look fashionable. Nastya told me about a friend of hers from Moscow who often went clubbing at night in a short skirt and busked in the street by day without gloves on. She contracted pneumonia and died in her mid-twenties; an early death for the sake of looking good on the dance floor.

The Mormon Invasion

There are a high number of Mormons in Krasnoyarsk. In the wake of the collapse of the USSR, they came in droves from ~~America~~ USA to preach their God stuff. Once they had set up a big church they started giving free English lessons as a way to attract people. Before we met, Nastya used to attend these English classes just for the practice, and though she quite enjoyed being part of the community and being able to speak English for an hour, she wasn't taken in by what she referred to as their 'fake smiles'.

Being a staunch existentialist, I'm uncomfortable listening to anything remotely religious. I think this has a lot to do with my father, who, when I was young, would shout abuse at the television during any news items related to religious affairs. Although I really loved singing hymns during school assembly back in the eighties, when I became a teenager, growing up in poverty in a seriously run down neighbourhood, the idea that some bearded holy man created everything 'for a reason' just didn't wash with me. Since then, much like my dad, if anyone talks to me about religious matters my ears automatically begin to switch off. Nastya usually had a lot of good things to say about her experiences with the Mormons, and made a great effort to convince me that they were a decent breed of people. We had to agree to disagree. However there were some points where we did see eye to eye: after each English lesson, the ~~American~~ US Mormons apparently give an hour's speech on gospel-related blah, and are normally very well dressed when they do this. Of course, these well turned out individuals attract a lot of attention. After all, they are foreigners, who are not only extremely polite and friendly, but smile when they talk. When a young Russian expresses a slight interest in the US they are then offered a private visit at home at a later date. However, instead of being visited by the actual person they spoke to, an 'elder' usually goes to their house with the intention of talking the curious person into joining the Mormons. This is, in part, due to the fact that it is forbidden for the US Mormons to have casual relations with the natives while on foreign missions. They are also not allowed to drink, smoke, or do any of the things I loved doing in my mid-twenties. When someone succumbs to the elder's pitch, they are then invited to become a member, where they get to attend regular gatherings. This so called fellowship doesn't come free. For a Russian person to join the Mormons they are encouraged to pay the minimum of 10 per cent of their income, which even Nastya could see was rather a lot of money.

As Nastya is still on good terms with the Mormons, despite having never joined up, we were invited to drink berry juice with one of her Mormon friends. During our meeting this Russian Mormon convert told me a controversial story that had happened about twenty years earlier. In the 1990s, when the Russian economy was at its lowest point, and security was a little lax, there was an incident involving a few US Mormon elders. Part of Krasnoyarsk is militarised, in the same way that part of St Athan in Wales is; and of course, while it's fine to walk in the non-militarised areas, it's completely illegal to walk through the gate into the military zone. Even so, this is precisely what the Mormon folk did, if they were indeed Mormons. When caught they gave the excuse that they had gone to preach 'the word' to the military. Apparently the barbwire and rows of electric fencing weren't big enough clues that they weren't welcome. This didn't wash with the Russians who quickly deported them. Thinking about it afterwards I wondered just how many of these Mormons were actually spies. It's the perfect cover. Mormons take particular care of their bodies, in the same way that the CIA do; it's not unusual for them to wander around annoying people by asking too many questions, plus they have access to special religious visas because they are sponsored by the church. I still can't help but smile to myself when I think of this story. There would have been no other way into that military complex, other than simply walking in. Those spies were either really arrogant, really desperate; or both.

Nastya, her parents, as well as a few of her friends and colleagues, told me that they thought the Mormon missionaries from America were mostly spies. Thinking about it, the notion that Americans would plant sleeper spies in Russia wasn't so farfetched. It wasn't so long ago that the British government was caught red-handed during the spy-rock-scandal of 2006. Left near a tree just outside Moscow, a fake rock was fitted with all the latest gadgetry that could send and receive information from spies as they walked past it, using small computers in their hands to interact with it. What the British didn't know was that they were being watched the whole time by the Federal Security Service of the Russian Federation (FSB). The affair became even more embarrassing when a video clearly showing British embassy staff walking past the rock, with eyes darting this way and that, was shown on Russian State TV. Following this there was the 2010 incident of ten Russian sleeper spies being discovered in the US, who included Anna Chapman, who became a national hero in Russia and a worldwide name. As a direct result of the discovery of spies in America there was another spy scandal, only this time it was a Russian accused of spying on the UK. In August 2010, Ekaterina Zatuliveter, a parliamentary aide to Mike Hancock,

MP for the Liberal Democrats, was accused by MI5 of being a Russian sleeper spy and faced deportation. Although she was later released without charge, it came to light during the investigation that Mike Hancock had asked many questions in the House of Commons related to Britain's nuclear weaponry; not only that but his office had requested information on the location of the entire British nuclear fleet, including an inventory of missiles.

In an interview with *The Guardian* on the 22nd of February 2012, retired KGB agent Boris Karpichkov said that even though the numbers of Russian intelligence personnel in London were expected to decrease at the end of the cold war; they didn't. Apparently, as Britain shifted its focus to the War on Terror, following the terrorist attack on ~~America~~ USA in 2001, Britain assumed the Russian intelligence community would scale back operations. Although there is absolutely no evidence to support such a claim, I wouldn't be surprised if it was proved true.

All of the incidents of spying listed above are due to what I call the unpublicised continuation of the cold war. Although the war was officially declared 'over' in 1991, and the Russians, ~~Americans~~ US and British agreed to stop stockpiling huge amounts of nuclear warheads in accordance with the already existing 'Non-Proliferation of Nuclear Weapons Treaty' (NPT), there is no treaty that I know of that asked countries to scale back their spying activities. Not only that but the vaguely worded NPT hasn't exactly brought about the disarmament of nuclear states, instead recognised nuclear states continue to upgrade and improve their nuclear arsenals citing threats from 'rogue states' as a reason not to disarm.

While I make it quite obvious I'm not overly fond of religious preaching, I have to say that the Russian Mormons extended the hand of friendship further than any of Nastya's other friends. While Nastya's old school mates and work colleagues were happy to talk to me when they visited us, I was rarely invited over to their apartments. The Russian Mormons on the other hand often invited me to their homes, where they offered me herbal tea and snacks. Not once did any of them talk to me about religion unless I asked, and even then they were tactful and never tried to convert me.

Christmas, Vodka and Snegurochka

Christmas and New Year are slightly different in Russia, compared with the West. December 25th isn't a major celebration at all as Russians prefer to celebrate Christmas on January 7th; according to the old Julian calendar. While they celebrate Christmas at a different time, New Year is still celebrated on December 31st, and then again there is a slightly smaller celebration on what is now known as 'Old New Year' on the eve of January 13th.

On December 25th, because I was used to some sort of festivity, Nastya took me to a place commonly known as Beaver Log, a ski resort on the south side of the river. To get there we took the bus, which dropped us off along the main road about a mile away from the resort. We then made our own way along the scenic route, which took us through a series of streets of what seemed to be the oldest dachas in Siberia. Once we reached the top of this district, we had to turn right, and walk towards the ski complex until we met an old wooden bridge. This bridge seemed to rise over a field of snow, and I wondered why it was that someone had taken the time to build a bridge when it wasn't needed. It took me a while to realise the field it passed over wasn't a field at all, but a river. The state-of-the-art Beaver Log complex also looked out of place opposite this dacha territory.

We took the ski lift to the top where there were several *shashlik* stands and hiking routes over the mountains. Past the cafés, we waded through knee-deep snowdrifts to where the authorities had set up a standing platform at the edge of the mountain's plateau. It looked out over several other mountains, all very much the same as the one we were stood on. With the entire city clearly visible behind us, it felt like we were on the very edge of civilisation; as if someone had drawn a line between life as I knew it, and no-man's-land. Beyond the barrier was wilderness on a scale I could not conceive. I reached my arm out as if to touch the trees in the distance, but that was as far as I was willing to go. After tea, *shashliks* and the obligatory photographs, we descended to where Nastya had arranged to meet her cousin Masha. In Russia, there is no differentiation between cousins and siblings, and so cousins are often referred to as sisters or brothers. Masha was someone I had met in Moscow during my first visit. Right before Nastya and I left on the Trans-Siberian we had met Masha, who was pregnant at the time, inside one of the metro stations. It had only been a fleeting introduction, as Masha was still working then. Now Masha had given birth to a baby boy named Kirill, she had come back to her home city to do some winter skiing, and to see her mum. Nastya and I were invited back to eat at her mother Lilya's place, and of course to see Kirill who was being looked after by Lilya while Masha was out skiing. Lilya's two sisters were also at the apartment and all three of them were cooking separate fish dishes. Nastya and I were very hungry by this point and weren't disappointed; because I was the first Welshman they had ever met, they wanted to make a good impression on me. I had to try every one of the fish dishes, no matter how full I was. I ate a bowl of fish soup, followed by fish salad, and a large slice of fish pie. By the end, I was so full I could have been rolled around like a snowball. It was Christmas Day to me, and I felt a kind of childish excitement inside, but it was obvious that to the rest of the company it was just another day. In the past I had criticised Christmas in Britain for being too commercial and full of obligation, which I still agree with, however, sitting in a small kitchen in Siberia, eating only fish, I couldn't help but miss my mother's overcooked Christmas dinner and all the unnecessary and unwanted gifts that had made Christmas Day a reason to celebrate.

On December 30th we were invited to join Nastya's work colleagues at her office for beer and cakes. It was a good opportunity to become acquainted with the people my wife spends forty-eight hours a week with and to see the place where she works. We walked for forty minutes to the nearest large shopping complex, where we stopped for wine and chocolates. Behind this shopping centre are several large factories, most of them heating factories that burn coal as part of the centralised heating systems. Among them is an old converted munitions factory that now houses offices, including Nastya's office. The entrance to this appears to be an old fire escape that is now converted to the main door. When I had a look at what is now the back of the building, I saw the original double doors were locked, bolted and never used. Around them hung a wrought iron archway with the hammer and sickle insignia, though the head of the hammer had rusted into nothing.

Inside the new entrance was a small box containing a security guard. Unlike the security guards I have known in offices back in the UK, this one sat watching TV, making occasional conversation with people he recognised. Apparently he was not employed to stop and check people's identity, because there wasn't an identity card system. He was simply there to make sure nobody walks out with anything under their arm and to intervene if any trouble happens.

We climbed the stairs to the second floor and Nastya led me through a wide doorway. Like every other building we had been in, including every small shop and supermarket, the floor was tiled and slippery. What made it worse were the snow grips I had attached to my boots to give me extra traction on the snow. I had to tread very carefully. That corridor could have been any other building in the city. There were no distinguishable features, save a few pictures on the wall of people on company outings. Like most other office buildings, the place was full of offices rented by several different companies, and there were very few signs on any doors to tell which was which. I was led through a door on the right, to a large room full of desks and at least twenty large computer towers with lights blinking. On the left were two doors, one that led to Nastya's office, which she shared with the boss, and the other had in it a leather sofa, a water dispenser, and a large glass cabinet that housed several computer memory boards complete with all the company secrets. A few of Nastya's colleagues were already there, mostly engineers and customer service workers. It was a pleasant evening, and we drank a lot. Everyone seemed to favour the beer and ignore the red wine, so I helped myself and got a bit merry. Normally, in any social situation I found it hard because my spoken Russian was pretty rubbish. Thankfully, two of the engineers spoke English well. I consumed enough alcohol to engage one of them, an ex-military man and ardent Putin supporter, in political debate. He was quite reasonable in his views on the apparent continuation of the cold war; he said things like 'There's no reason two superpowers can't get along and be friends. They shouldn't feel like they constantly have to engage each other just because they are powerful.' Wise words indeed.

After far too much alcohol had been consumed, and all the cake had magically disappeared, the security guard, who was apparently worried there was a Westerner sat drinking in the room full of company secrets, came and asked us to go. Everyone shook hands and left. Both Nastya and I were pretty drunk by this point, and in our infinite wisdom thought it would be fun to try and walk home. It was close to midnight, -30 °C and we had trouble trying to keep from singing. Our plan was to go home and sleep off the booze but the night didn't go that way. Dima, on his way back from a company party in the centre, noticed us on his drive home and pulled over. Marina was with him and had a large pink cake she had pilfered from the party. She brought it out of the car, placed it on the cover of the boot and motioned to me try some. It was clear she was as pissed as me. We both dug in with our hands and scoffed as much as we could manage, covering our faces in pink icing. It was another of life's beautiful moments. Dima seemed to think it would be a good idea for Nastya and I to go to their place and continue drinking. Not a wise move but it seemed like a good idea at the time.

We drove to their apartment, conveniently only two miles south of where we lived. It was nice inside; they'd had it repaired to a pretty high standard, although like Nastya's parents, Dima and Marina slept in the living room because their one designated bedroom was lived in by Semka and his giant indoor climbing frame. The kitchen was also smaller than Nataliya Petrovna's, but it was just big enough for the four of us to sit down around the small table. We drank, we drank and we ate. Marina was trying hard to make a good impression, so I got to eat from the jar of pickled mushrooms which were her favourite food. I also tried *pelmeni* for the first time, having been a bit afraid of trying it before. It wasn't as bad as I thought it would be. Though a bit salty and a bit slimy, it was very similar to ravioli, except it wasn't served with any sauce and instead of being square, each parcel is round and looks more like a bowl of cream eyeballs. Marina explained that Russians offer many foods when they have guests, but when the guests are gone the hosts always cook *pelmeni* for themselves as it's cheap, and very easy to cook. *Pelmeni* is to the Russians what rarebit is to the Welsh. All was going well until the vodka and cognac came out. As a Westerner, Russian vodka etiquette wasn't something ingrained in me. I forgot to eat something after each shot, and there were many shots. The bottles had to be finished or we would suffer some sort of bad luck.

I was woken the following day by Dima at 6 p.m. Nastya had left earlier because she was annoyed at me for throwing up the night before. I had the worst hangover. Worse than any I had known at any other point in my life. I was in Semka's bed; fortunately he had stayed with his grandparents for the night. Marina forced some soup down my neck and I had a shower. I felt disgusting. At 8 p.m. Dima drove me home to where Nastya was waiting for me. We had planned to celebrate New Year's Eve with Nataliya Petrovna at her friend Lilya's apartment, as Boris was out on a hunt and Nataliya Petrovna didn't want to be stuck at home with only Baba Ira for company. Nastya was thoroughly pissed off with me. I changed quickly and we made our way by taxi to the east of the city where Lilya lived with her granddaughter, also named Nastya. Lilya's apartment was quite like the other Lilya's I had visited on Christmas Day. It was very well decorated. In fact I would say it was posh. There were many rooms, a giant sofa, an equally giant television, and the kitchen looked horribly expensive. Lilya was an accountant and liked to buy only things of the best quality. I was afraid to touch the plates and because the crystal glass looked so expensive I gripped it like it was some kind of precious sculpture, strong enough not to let it go, but careful not to crush it.

In keeping with Russian etiquette, it was my job as the man to pour champagne. I had terribly shaky hands, a chronic hangover, and every glass was worth more than all the money I had in my wallet. I drank juice all night, except for one glass of champagne at midnight. When the changing of the year struck, Putin gave a speech on TV, and was on most of the channels. Out the window, because we were ten floors up, we could see hundreds of fireworks. The New Year's celebration is so huge, and there are so many fireworks for so long because Russia is nine time zones big. At the stroke of midnight, nine times consecutively, a different part of Russia begins to celebrate. It used to be eleven; however in March 2010 The Kremlin abolished two time zones, one in the far west of Russia and one in the far east. Apparently so many time zones had a negative impact on the economy. A year later, daylight saving time was also abolished. Before I left for Russia in the summer, Moscow was three hours ahead of the UK, but when the clocks went back in the UK in October, Moscow was ahead of Greenwich Mean Time (GMT) by four hours. All very confusing when you're booking flights often, and annoying when I was in the UK because I was used to calling Nastya at 5 p.m. GMT as it was 12 p.m. KRAT (Krasnoyarsk time), usually to say goodnight. After the clocks went back if I called Nastya at 5 p.m., she would get annoyed because it was 1 a.m. KRAT and she would already be sleeping.

At 1 a.m. Nastya and I left for home in a taxi, leaving Nataliya Petrovna and Lilya dancing to a pop concert on the TV. Nastya had a day shift the next day and needed to be up at 6:30 a.m. I was glad of this because I was desperate for a proper night's sleep and my hangover wanted to avoid the inevitable karaoke.

Red Tape

From December 31st to January 7th Russia comes to a full stop to allow room for the New Year hangover. It is the largest national holiday of the year. After the revolution of 1917, most of the traditions that were originally associated with Christmas, like Grandfather Frost, were moved to New Year's Eve because the Soviet leaders (being devout atheists) wanted to steer clear of anything remotely Christian. Because of this, Christmas trees in Russia are known as New Year Trees. The relationship between Russia and tree decoration goes back to the 17th Century when Peter the Great, the man in charge at the time, decided it would be a good idea to introduce Christmas trees to Russia after he had seen them in Western Europe while on his holidays. All was well until

1916, when indoor trees were banned because the tradition had originated from Germany, and the Russians were pissed off with the Germans over World War I. This ban continued until 1935, when a letter calling for Christmas trees to be reinstated was published in a communist newspaper. To avoid the religious element, Christmas trees were rebranded as New Year trees and because they no longer had anything to do with God they were allowed back into people's apartments. They even went so far as to allow Santa Claus back into the country (though I'm not sure what visa he had).

The modern tradition of having a day off work after New Year began in the late forties and was originally called non-labour day. This was later extended to five days, but, with Christmas Day on the 7th and old New Year on the 13th, the holiday was unofficially extended by the will of the people so it could include both Christmas and New Year's parties. By this time I had become an ardent reader of *The Moscow Times*, the only daily English-language newspaper in Russia, and was really surprised to see an article that implied 'see you when the partying stops'.

After the New Year party at Lilya's, Nastya and I started to lean towards the idea of me moving to Russia permanently. We were tired of saying goodbye so often; the way we were living simply wasn't right. We spent some of the holiday period researching Russian immigration policy; there was a lot to learn and if it was anything like obtaining a visa, we had to get it exactly right and perfectly timed when I applied for documents. To become a permanent resident, I first needed to obtain temporary residency. To get this I needed a private visa, which could only be obtained through Nastya formally inviting me to Russia with some lengthy letter obtained through the immigration office, stamped a hundred and one times and validated by a stamp that is the boss of all other stamps. After this invitation and all the stamps were issued, it then needed to be submitted, along with passport, photos, and all other relevant blah to the Russian embassy in London. When the immigrant had re-entered Russia on their private visa they then needed to submit a criminal records certificate, with Apostille, translated and notarised, with two completed temporary residency forms, a notarised translated copy of the person's passport, a notarised copy of something else, written consent of everyone currently living in Russia, written consent of everyone living outside of Russia, a chest X-ray certificate, a leprosy certificate and a partridge in a pear tree to the official Russian Office of Comings and Goings. On top of this, all the medical tests must have been performed at clinics specified by the Office of Comings and Goings and must have been validated by at least two thousand and fifty six stamps, which all had to be the exact same shade of pink and all had to overlap each other one tenth of an inch. In fact, the real list of requirements was ten times longer, but I've cut it short as it adds fifty more pages to this book. The only thing I needed to worry about initially was the criminal records certificate. I searched online for the right place to get one and, on the website of the Russian embassy in London, I found a page dedicated to non-criminal records certificates for immigration purposes. Bingo.

Aeroflot Flight SU2571. May 28th 2012. London — Moscow

My flight back to London in winter had gone without a hitch and before I knew it I was in Cardiff. As I had got my eight hours back that I had lost on the way to Siberia, I had arrived in Cardiff at about 6 p.m. I was still wearing Boris's spare black hunting jacket and his ushanka of real mink fur. Carrying my half-empty suitcase over my shoulder, I bought a train ticket to Llantwit Major and stood on platform 6 of Cardiff Central Station. I was aware of how Russian I looked but didn't care because people seemed to give me a wide berth, which I enjoyed. Not only that but I felt Russian; I was Michael Oliver of Krasnoyarsk, with a lovely Siberian wife to go home to, a dacha to enjoy in the summer, and the knowledge that I would soon be returning to Siberia for good. I stood with my shoulders back, chest out and head high. When I reached Llantwit Major however I quickly removed my ushanka and stuffed it into my suitcase as I had to walk for thirty minutes to my mother's house in St Athan. She lives a gunshot away from RAF St Athan's main gate and the approach to my mother's is always overlooked by an armed soldier with a semi-automatic weapon; I didn't want him to think the Russians were invading.

I spent a fortnight getting used to British life again, although it didn't really take much getting used to. I ate more full breakfasts than were good for me and indulged in half a billion packets of salt and vinegar crisps. Russian crab flavoured 'chips' for some reason just don't give me the same satisfaction. By early February it was high time to pay the Russian embassy in London a visit.

The opening time of the department that dealt with certificate requests was 8.45 a.m., and it closed just three hours later. I needed to be in London early. The only way I could do this was by taking the National Express at 4.30 a.m. There was no way I could get to the station easily at that hour from my dad's house in Ely, or my mum's place in Llantwit Major. Once again I called upon the services of my mate Torben, who insisted we have ten pints in the pub followed by double shots of whatever he had left in his kitchen.

Red Paint

When I arrived in London, I wasn't as hung-over as I thought I would have been but I was still suffering a little. After going to the wrong address and being given directions by two policemen, I arrived at the embassy five minutes before they opened. Having had all my visas arranged for me by a private visa firm based in London, I hadn't actually seen the Russian embassy before, even though I had already visited Russia three times. It looked different to how I imagined because it was covered in blotches of red paint. Though the majority of the building was a nice clean cream colour, most of the windows, ledges and stonework – from the ground up to the third floor – were smeared in thick red gloss. It was clear it had been paint-bombed in the not too distant past.

During the Russian elections on December 4th, the United Russia party won an absolute majority of seats in the Duma with 49.32 per cent of the vote, however, there were reports of election fixing and many people felt that the system had utterly failed them. Just three months prior to the elections, at the United Russia Party Congress held in Moscow on September 24th, Russian President Dmitry Medvedev proposed that his predecessor, Vladimir Putin, stand for the presidency in 2012; an offer which Putin accepted. In return, Putin offered to nominate Medvedev for the role of prime minister. Many people felt that everything had been decided well in advance, meaning the elections had been a pointless show. There were growing concerns that by keeping power in the hands of the same men who had led Russia for the past four years it would lead to political and economic stagnation. It did seem like a strange situation. The choice only came down to two men, and those same men simply swapped roles as if nobody's opinion or vote mattered and, of course, this led to widespread dissent and protests. While I was in Russia, I hadn't paid too much attention to the elections because I had only one month to spend with my wife, and as a Westerner, it didn't seem like my business. I'm not saying people don't have the right to criticise the policies of any foreign nation, but I believe one should exercise caution when criticising a country they are attempting to gain permission to live in. Not only that but it seemed hypocritical of me to berate Russia when the state of British politics wasn't much better.

On December 10th, Russia experienced its biggest protests since the fall of the Soviet Union; not just in Moscow but right across the country, in eighty-eight towns and cities including Krasnoyarsk. At the time of the demonstration, Nastya and I had kept away from the city centre, firstly because Nastya is politically apathetic, and secondly because the British Foreign Office website advised that it wouldn't be easy to help me if I got into trouble, even if I only went as a spectator. Protests were simultaneously held near Russian embassies across the globe, including London. Looking at that red paint it struck me how sheltered I had been; there had been so many outcries and yet I had barely seen or heard anything while I was in Russia. It also really awakened me to the possibility of there being further social and political instability in Russia, and to the fact that Putin was going to become president once again. Even though United Russia is widely seen as Putin's party I had so far only visited Siberia while Medvedev was in power. I began to worry about immigration policy when Putin took the reins. Would they let me in? This was coupled with the fact that I had written several poems over the past year that would probably never be popular with the Kremlin. In one poem I had even criticised the trial of Mikhail Khodorkovsky, a man who openly argued with Putin on television and who subsequently found himself in prison. I had sent this poem off with several others of similar style and theme to a competition that I had a decent chance of winning. Before submitting them however, Nastya had insisted on censoring certain lines, which annoyed me at the time but, with hindsight, I could see that she was just trying to keep me safe.

After queuing for five minutes, I was ushered into the grounds of the embassy by a security official who I suspected wasn't Russian because he smiled when he spoke to people. This was confirmed when I saw him dealing with people asking him questions at the gate. He didn't seem to speak much Russian but spoke English perfectly. He was actually quite a nice addition to the embassy staff and made my visit a much less intimidating experience. Inside the embassy I was given a ticket and ushered into a waiting room. The interior guard didn't speak English and couldn't understand my piss-poor Russian. Inside the waiting room were several other Russians. From the way they dressed they couldn't have been anything else. The decor was also Russian and a stark contrast to the English architecture on the exterior of the building. It was like being sat in the living room of the apartment in Krasnoyarsk. There was even a television showing old Russian films. The number of my ticket came up almost immediately as I was the only person there waiting to apply for a certificate, so I left the room and was ushered by the security guard into a space that resembled a Russian post office. An attractive middle-aged woman took my certificate request from me, which was a standard form I had printed from their website, and in basic English told me I would be 'contacted'.

Leaving the embassy I wondered just how contact would be made as there had been no sections on the form for me to add a phone number or email address; the only address it had asked for and the one I had provided was for the apartment in Krasnoyarsk.

White Paint

On February 19th I received an email from the adjudicator of the competition I had submitted my poems to in January. Of the six poems I had entered, four of them had been selected for publication in June. These were 'After the Cold War', a poem written during my first visit to Russia detailing my frustration with the relationship between Britain and Russia; 'There are no problems in Russia', a poem that lists every problem in Russia I could think of, including the trial of Khodorkovsky; 'Red', a poem about my encounter with the Topol-M missiles in Moscow; and 'Anthropogenic', a self-critical poem, but one that lists certain atrocities by humans I have never fought or protested against, including a controversial factory being built near Krasnoyarsk. I had been awarded second prize. While this was good news, it also meant that certain poems that were openly critical of aspects of Russian politics and leadership would be in the public domain. Damage control was needed.

Just three days before, I had secured publication of an anti-English monarchy poem in an anthology titled *Poems for a Welsh Republic*, scheduled for release in June also. I had toyed with the idea of writing a sister poem to 'There are no problems in Russia' but had not done so because I had been so busy travelling back and forth to Siberia and working as much as possible in between. I quickly drafted 'There are no problems in the United Kingdom' and sent it to many friends, including the editor of *Poems for a Welsh Republic*, disguised as a work in progress I could use some help with. It was accepted the same day. I wasn't too concerned about my Russia-themed poems being out there – I was a little-known Welsh poet with a small readership, and as such I was sure that nobody had heard of me in Russia. I could safely assume that the Kremlin would never be aware that these poems existed, but if they did read them and took a dislike to them I could then point them in the direction of the sister poem that criticised the political system and monarchy of the UK. *But not wales.*

I was probably being a bit paranoid but so much depended on me being granted Russian residency that I could leave nothing to chance. I was caught between writing and publishing exactly what I felt I needed to, and the idea that I should suppress my writing until I had everything sorted. Unfortunately, I've never been good at thinking things through before I do them, and if I'm advised not to do something, it makes me want to do it even more. Although those poems never caused me any problems, with hindsight I can see that I should have put my ego in a box, thrown all my poems on the fire and concentrated on what I should have been doing with regard to residency papers. Or as Nastya might say: 'only a fool and a complete arsehole puts publishing before the needs of his wife.'

Just two days after I received the acceptance email, five members of the Russian punk band Pussy Riot performed a 40-second anti-Kremlin song in Moscow's Cathedral of Christ the Saviour. This cathedral was destroyed under Soviet rule and rebuilt in the 1990s; which made it a very significant place for people to say their prayers. Within the next few weeks, three of the group were arrested for 'hooliganism motivated by religious hatred' while two others fled Russia. The detention and trial of the arrested trio became a source of controversy causing worldwide public outcry. The Russian reaction was quite the opposite of that in the West. Russian people, for the most part, take their religion and associated places of worships very seriously. It came as no surprise to me that while the West was outraged by the arrest of the three punk poppers, the majority of

Russians were outraged by the punk prayer actions of Pussy Riot, and subsequently annoyed by the hysteria in the West. The problem was that while the protest was clearly political, the fact that they made their protest in a church opened them up to being viewed as anti-religious. The majority of Russians I spoke to after said they weren't offended by the protest itself, but by the fact the singers showed a complete disregard for the regular, everyday folk who attended that particular church. Their actions were seen as a show of hostility, not against the government, but against the Orthodox community. Had they protested in Red Square, or sang their song in a club or protest rally, it's likely they would never have been arrested and we might never have heard of them. But then the whole point of their protest was to highlight Putin's relationship with the Orthodox Church. In recent years the Kremlin and the Church seem to have become so entangled that Patriarch Kirill, the head of the Orthodox Church in Russia, has claimed that Putin's government had performed a 'miracle of God', by stabilising the country after the economic struggles during the 1990s. He later openly supported Putin before the 2012 elections, which would definitely have influenced the vote seeing as three-quarters of the Russian population register as being Orthodox Christians. Besides this, the Orthodox Church has publicly supported the Kremlin so often and in so many ways that they have even been recorded blessing Russian rockets.

Choosing Moscow's Christ the Saviour as their protest point worked both for and against Pussy Riot. The Kremlin and the media they controlled were able to spin the event to make it seem as if the band were anti-Orthodox, not anti-Kremlin. Putin later accused the group of threatening 'the moral foundations of Russia', while others accused them of 'blasphemy', 'being in league with Satan' and/or 'some Americans'. This led to a popular view that if you were a supporter of Pussy Riot you must therefore be an enemy of the church; consequently the focus shifted away from the actual message Pussy Riot members were trying to convey. However, the way the people saw 'Putin' and 'the church' as the same entity perfectly exemplified the dangerous relationship Pussy Riot had sought to highlight.

When I first heard of their arrest I shared the same view as those in the West; I couldn't see that Pussy Riot had committed an actual crime. No one was hurt and their song had lasted less than a minute. As a counter PR stunt, I thought it would have looked good for Putin if the trio were set free; however he would then have had to face a backlash of criticism and outrage from his own people. It was a political catch-22. I also wondered about Pussy Riot themselves. While their punk pop song had achieved the desired effect in the West, successfully promoting a hatred of Putin, they must have known they would be arrested and sent to prison. Even I knew how sacred the church is to Russia, having been turned away following an attempt to take photographs inside one of our local churches in Krasnoyarsk. If I had waltzed in with my guitar and sung something as harmless even as the *SpongeBob SquarePants* theme tune, I would have been arrested and would probably have ended up doing some time in prison. I also knew that if someone wanted to effect a change in Russian politics, singing punk pop probably wouldn't have any lasting effect, and yet their forty-second song was much more effective in turning the world's gaze towards Russia than any poem could ever be. In the age of the pop song and the soundbite, I realise that music was probably their best vehicle of communication, though I can't help but be cautious of pop-star revolutionaries; everyone thought the Sex Pistols were the antidote to the capitalist model of art, right up until one of them started making adverts for Country Life Butter.

When I spoke to Nastya on the phone about the Pussy Riot situation, she said she didn't sympathise with them at all as their actions had only affected churchgoers and hadn't had any effect whatsoever on anyone else. Her friends shared a similarly unsympathetic view, as it seemed did the majority of the Russian populace, their outrage spilling onto many online comments forums. 'An opinion poll of Russians released by the independent Levada research group showed only 6 per cent had sympathy with the women' while '51 per cent said they found nothing good about them'. This bad feeling was reported by the Western media, who spun it by stating that most Russians got their information from television, and therefore swallowed the state's official opinion, since many TV stations in Russia are state-owned. This was quite offensive as it insinuated Russians couldn't think for themselves. I knew Nastya didn't swallow anything fed to the general populace through the TV, neither did most of her friends; they got their news from multiple sources via the internet. Nastya formed her view of the band after watching a pro-Pussy Riot video on YouTube.

At the same time, there came a stream of Pussy Riot support messages online, and petitions in the West calling for their release. Every man and his dog in the West joined the 'I'm with the brave people' campaign, even Sting, the saviour of the rainforests who went on to make a car advertisement. I couldn't help but wonder that if Western celebrities really supported Pussy Riot, why didn't they fly to Moscow, ditch their passport and security staff and start a march up and down Red Square. But that would never happen, because while it became cool to support Pussy Riot, those celebrities in the West simply wanted to be seen as an 'activist' without actually being active. Though this can't be said of Tilda Swinton who later took to Moscow's Red Square with a rainbow flag in protest against Russia's recent 'gay propaganda law', yet another source of contention between Russia and the rest of the world. 'I support Pussy Riot' became a cool slogan, a bit like those people that wear Che Guevara t-shirts, most of whom love to wear the logo but would never have opted to fight for the freedom of the people and give their lives in a Bolivian jungle by Che's side. In the West, while it was cool to talk about Pussy Riot, other people's causes were going unnoticed. For example, far fewer people made petitions to save the poet Talha Ahsan, a British poet who had been held in custody in the UK without trial or charge since 2006, after being accused by the ~~Americans~~ *USA* of contributing to illegal 'terrorist' websites. The case was very similar to that of Gary McKinnon, the British computer genius who famously hacked the NASA database to seek evidence of UFOs. Like Mr McKinnon, Talha Ahsan is on the Asperger's Spectrum, however despite this common factor it was only Ahsan who ended up being extradited to the US.

According to the Russian embassy website, criminal record certificates can take up to six months to process. After emailing to check on progress I was informed that mine was ready just five weeks after I had applied. A week later, after another night at Torben's flat, I woke up in London on the National Express. I had a vague memory of beer, singing and of Torben putting an omelette in my one hand and a cup of coffee in the other, before pointing to the station and telling me to 'walk that way'. I made it to the embassy in time to pick up my certificate and was coherent enough to thank them in Russian pronounced so badly that it made everyone laugh. When I left the building I noticed the red paint was hardly visible. It was now a very light pink after someone had attempted a whitewash with emulsion. Not only was the new white a lighter shade than the rest of the building, but the mark left by the earlier protests was still visible beneath the fresh paint, a sign perhaps that Putin's opposition couldn't be extinguished so easily.

Visas and the Capitalist Mclympics

As I left London on the coach, I wrote out several postcards for Nastya. This was something I had done routinely since March

x are these 'legal' terrorist web sites

2009, and I estimated that I had sent over five hundred. It cost a fortune in stamps but I felt it was an essential form of physical communication during times when we couldn't physically be together. When I got back to Cardiff, I spoke with Nastya of my success at having obtained the first certificate necessary for us to be able to spend our lives together. She had even better news. Not only had she obtained the invitation for my private visa but her parents had gifted us a hefty portion of their savings. This money coupled with a small mortgage meant we could buy our own flat: Nastya planned to go out flat hunting with Boris that very week and it was likely that they would buy one before my arrival and partly furnish it so that I wouldn't have to sleep on the floor when I got there. We arranged my visa for the end of May and bought a return flight package from Aeroflot. We opted for return tickets as the immigration process for temporary residency took five months, and a private visa was only valid for three.

I spent the next two months working as much as possible. I aimed my poetry submissions well and had a few decently paid performances. With the money I made I bought several Cadbury Easter eggs, twelve Chocolate Oranges and fistfuls of Fry's Chocolate Creams for Nastya. To prevent Semka from watering at the mouth with jealousy, I also bought a stash of Olympic medal chocolates and chocolate tools from the old sweet shop in Cardiff's Royal Arcade. I was slightly sad that I would be missing the Olympics. When I was a boy, my dad and I used to sit together and watch them on the telly; he even knew most of the athletes' names. I was only slightly comforted by the fact that my dad probably wouldn't even enjoy it. The Tory government was turning the event into the most commercial Olympic Games ever, going so far as to introduce draconian laws that would ensure people only ate food supplied by the official sponsors McDonalds while only being able to pay for their cardboard meals with a Visa card; two things my dad hates. My dad, like many people born

Libel. All sponsors are organised by the International Olympic Organisation, nothing to do with home government. He is a soviet agent.

134

in the 1950s has a habit of taking a packed lunch with him wherever he goes and doesn't like being forced into parting with hard-earned money. Still, I was disappointed for him, as he would probably have bought tickets and realised a lifelong dream had the Olympics been about sport, as it had been when he was a boy.

This feeling of missing out on an important bonding session with my dad had been exacerbated at Heathrow. While waiting to board my flight to Russia, I was surrounded not only by advertisements for the Olympics, but as I was leaving the country to begin the residency process abroad, hoards of people were entering the country to see the Olympic games. I even passed a few teams. Sat on the plane I thought of all the things my dad and I would never do together. We had always been close. No matter how many fights we had fought in the past, and there were many of those, we had always managed to build new bridges. We were after all two halves of the same person. Our faces have always been very similar; we have always liked the same music and over the years, we have included each other in whatever we could. My dad had never failed to come to my book launches, poetry readings and birthday parties. We had spent countless times in the Brecon Beacons, on walking and cycling trips. After my parents divorced, I had gone with him on many of his annual caravan holidays, where we stayed up late talking through family stuff while gorging on junk food. Now I was flying to the other half of the world, planning to move there permanently, with a suitcase full of my dad's favourite Chocolate Oranges. For everything gained in life a sacrifice had to be made; this is what I had been told many years earlier by the very man who (I only then realised) was the big sacrifice I was making. For many years, I had blamed my parents for my slow start in life, for not being able to go to university, not achieving my full potential; the list goes on and on. It's true to some degree, because we were very poor, and my parents didn't have much of a clue when they made me and my sisters; yet from the point I had met Nastya it was my parents who had helped me out immeasurably. They let me sleep at their places, let me eat their food, my dad helped me get work, or he gave me money if I was short. For all the times in my life I could pinpoint and say 'that's where they let me down', they had since made up for by being there when I needed them the most. And I was leaving them, without saying so much as thank you.

PART IV

Aeroflot Flight SU1481. August 25th 2012. Krasnoyarsk — Moscow

I was worried we wouldn't make the plane in time. I really appreciated that Masha had agreed to fly to Moscow on the same flight as me but, after waking up at 4.30 a.m. to get to the airport two hours early, when Masha arrived just five minutes before boarding I had to bite my tongue to keep from being hurtfully sarcastic. Masha had this way of not caring too much about timekeeping. It wasn't arrogance, because she was never late, yet she never seemed to rush anywhere or feel the need to be anywhere early. After final tearful hugs with Nastya, Masha and I said goodbye to the entire family and entered the departure lounge of Yemelyanovo. When our flight number was called, still being unable to understand Russian, Masha got up and sprang towards the exit leaving me behind. I followed to where she was stood at the back of the queue. When the attendant motioned to open the gate, Masha called out that she had her baby boy and should therefore be allowed on the flight first. It worked. She parted the crowd carrying Kirill and I followed with the pushchair. Sat on the plane, I suspected that had been Masha's plan all along. I wondered how many times she had used her status as a young mum to push to the front of a queue, or as an excuse for her own lack of punctuality. At the same time I couldn't help but admire her audacity. She was courageous – I suppose she needed to be as I had never seen her with her husband, who, as quite an important scientist, didn't have any free time to visit his in-laws with his wife. I had only seen pictures of him on VKontakte, the Russian social network. I wanted to ask Masha about how she felt, with her husband being so busy, but I couldn't as we were sat on different ends of the plane.

It was my last flight out of Krasnoyarsk, or it would be if I played my cards right. I couldn't afford to make another error with the certificates. It had been a real blow finding out my two trips to the Russian embassy in London had been absolutely pointless. They hadn't come cheap – I had spent roughly £100 each time for travel, food and Tube rates. Not the most costly error but still, I had no room in my budget to allow for another one. This time I had to get it right, or my last flight out of Krasnoyarsk would become my last-but-one. We were so close to finally being able to live together in the same country permanently, under the same roof with never a need for me to leave again. I felt determined I could make it happen, and felt very sure of myself for the first time in a very adult way. The summer had changed me. Our new apartment had changed me. I had tasted the life I wanted and lived it for a full three months. Being just one certificate away from legal residency, our entire future was in my hands, just like Kirill's entire future sat in Masha's hands. Thinking about it, Masha's attitude was something I needed to emulate. With so much at stake it wouldn't hurt to become as self-assured as her, and determined to the point that I didn't see other people before me, or queues, or bureaucracy, just obstacles that I would treat with complete disregard. Still, I was comforted by the knowledge that the hard work was behind me. The right wheels were in motion because I had set them in motion, plus I had a definite place on earth I could now call home.

Summer, Liberty and Leprosy

During my early twenties I had been a bit of a loner. A serious love affair from the age of sixteen had left me heartbroken. Consequently I didn't have any girlfriends between the age of twenty and twenty five, because I was still nursing my broken heart. As I had nobody to spend my money on, I bought a lot of things for myself including jewellery. I even went through a phase of designing some individual pieces. While some of my male friends thought this was a bit effeminate I didn't care because I learned a great deal about the jewellery-making business while accumulating quite a handsome collection of one-of-a-kind rings. On a few of my previous trips to Russia I had noticed that quite a few Russian men also wore rings. Not just wedding rings but elaborate silver rings with huge rubies. These men were always very well-dressed with smart suit jackets and shiny shoes. As it was approaching summer and there was no pressing need to dress for the snow or extreme heat, I tidied myself up properly before leaving Wales. Regardless of the fact I wore trainers, with my tan leather coat and three ruby rings I looked quite similar to some of the wealthier Russians I had seen on previous flights. It had the desired effect. Aeroflot's flight attendants treated me better although they had never been unkind before, and I sailed through customs like a fish on a water slide. By the time I reached Krasnoyarsk I felt like a king. This illusion was quickly shattered when my luggage returned to me on the conveyor belt inside Yemelyanovo airport. It had gotten stuck somewhere and because it was made of thin material, had turned into a ball of ribbons with Chocolate Oranges inside. Clutching my stash I was met at the airport by Nastya and Boris who drove us back to our new apartment.

Unable to be far away from her family, Nastya had bought us an apartment just down the road from her parents' place. Our building didn't look as modern as theirs from the outside, and was ten storeys tall as opposed to their five. It was made with large grey bricks and had much smaller balconies. It sat in close proximity to another building of similar design, with a mishmash of square concrete slabs and messy sections of grass separating the two, plus a single rusty old children's swing from the Soviet years.

The design of the building meant that our apartment was west facing, with a balcony that looked across to the neighbouring building and down onto the communal square. We had been spoilt by the view of mountains over Semka's school back at Nastya's parents' place. Another difference was that there were two entrances: one east, one west. We were on the western side, where it was easier to park cars. Nastya opened the main door with her magnetic key, and it was clear that it wasn't any kind of palace. It looked like it should have been condemned a decade earlier. The foyer floor was a soup of cigarette butts and empty bottles. The walls were grey through years of abuse and from grubby hand prints. Despite all this I managed to see a bright side; our building did have one plus point, a lift – a 4 ft by 4 ft box, with heavy steel buttons, dulled from decades of jabbing fingers. There were more bottles and cigarette butts here too and some kind of fluid – a mix of blood and spilled beer – giving it an exceptionally grubby feel, which wasn't helped by the strip lights that blinked off and on. It reminded me of scenes from horror films, where the ghost of a small girl would appear every time the light went off. God only knows what had taken place in that lift over the years. It was a tight squeeze stuffing ourselves in there with my suitcase, but we managed and Nastya pressed the fifth button. The lift's one redeeming feature was its speed. The doors closed as soon as Nastya touched the button, which meant it was good in emergencies. At this point, I could imagine many scenarios where I might want to exit this building and fast.

On the fifth floor Nastya led Boris and me into a long corridor. Ours was the last door on the right, and boasted a front door that was built with love. It was built to stop tanks, armies and even Godzilla should it decide to try breaking in. I made a tremendous noise as I approached. On the ground were six subfloor access panels between our front door and the foyer – flat steel squares sat on square holes in the floor. Nastya and Boris had obviously made a note of where they were and avoided them, even though the hallway was only lit by one small bulb.

Once inside the apartment, we had a cup of English tea with milk. By request I had brought a variety of teas from Marks & Spencer, and Nastya had already bought a pouch of milk before coming to collect me. I say a pouch because not all milk in Russia comes in cartons. To save money, milk can be bought in plastic pouches; these are then plopped into a plastic pouch holder that looks like a funny sort of beaker with a large handle. We didn't have a beaker, so we simply leant our milk pouch against something else in the fridge to stop it from spilling everywhere. Calmed by a nice cuppa I decided our apartment was quite homely. Though it was a great deal smaller than what we had been used to it seemed lighter. Just off our hallway complete with little coat hooks was the kitchen with a new fridge-freezer, and a small balcony connected to it, which, though it had closed blinds, filled our kitchen with natural light. Our bedroom on the other side of the wall was the length of the kitchen and hallway combined. It had red satin curtains that bunched up against the floor because they were too long. Nastya had borrowed them from a friend of hers, as we couldn't afford our own yet. They added to the feeling of homeliness because they were very similar to the red velvet curtains my parents used to hang in the living room when I was a boy. My mum and dad had fought over them so many times. Mum wanted them open but dad wanted them closed. He had grown quite paranoid over the years. Often I would come home from school to find him stood at the curtains, open just a fraction so he could peer out and see who was lurking nearby. We had a gulley next to the house and sometimes people would hide there. When nobody was looking, they would come out and siphon the petrol out of my dad's van. No one ever caught them at it and my dad must have wasted hundreds of hours over the years peering through the little slit. When children were walking home from school my dad would stand there and watch them go, just in case one of them threw stones at his vehicle, which had happened only once before. The absence of light in the living room made it quite a depressing place to be, especially in my teenage years. Countless times I can remember coming home from a gig in my late teens only to trip over my parents' feet as they slept on the floor. It was worse after the divorce. Long after everyone had left except my dad, I would go to visit him on Saturdays. The split had a terribly negative effect on him and for several years he insisted on a complete absence of light, even going as far as to nail the curtains closed permanently. It took years of visits and coaxing him out before he finally let the light back in. My dad and Boris were actually alike in many ways. While my dad hated putting old bills in the bin in case someone stole his identity, Boris was afraid of the internet, saying 'It's a military invention.' Though I found both their attitudes humorous to begin with, I can't say that either of them was wrong. Coming from the USSR, Boris was unusually paranoid about people he or his family had contact with. If Nastya had any sort of interaction with someone Boris would ask, 'Who are they? Why do they want to know you? What is their agenda?' Occasionally his suspicious nature rubbed off on me and I had to be careful not to be overly inquisitive of every new person who entered my life.

Unfortunately, with another identical building just across the square with balconies and bedrooms that looked over at ours, our curtains had to remain closed most of the time. This made me feel that no matter how far from my family I lived, I would never be able to escape certain patterns of behaviours, and I would need to be careful not to fall into the same trap my father had.

During the first two weeks back in Siberia there wasn't any time to get settled in. Nastya had a fortnight off work, and we thought it best to get all the immigration stuff out of the way as soon as possible. Firstly, we had to register my visa. As it was my first private visa I thought it would need to be registered at the Federal Migration Service (UFMS), but the post office didn't question us when we went there and registered me anyway. It was the usual headache: forms had to be completed perfectly; we had to give photocopies of my passport pages, immigration card, copies of Nastya's residence papers, copies of the declaration of human rights (handwritten), forty-nine thousand copies of my finger prints, prints of my arse, and a brain scan. As usual, Nastya made a small mistake on one of the forms so we had to go to the photocopy shop to make more, fill these in, and go back. Like most previous occasions, registering took more than an hour of fussing about, queuing and going from place to place. This was the easy part.

Obtaining the chest X-ray certificate should have been simple – we just needed to make an appointment by phone and go to the hospital at the right time. Only the hospital was indistinguishable from every other building and it took ages to find. Eventually inside we registered, paid and then headed to the basement to wait for the nurse to show up. We were the only people there waiting for this service. Once the nurse came I had to get my shirt off, stand inside a machine, wait a second, and then it was all over. The nurse wrote something on a piece of paper, which we took and handed into one of the previous desks to get my certificate. It was only when I had it in my hand that I saw I didn't have TB; for some reason the nurse couldn't tell me beforehand, which was a bit nerve wracking. I was quite relieved. Not that I had any symptoms of any sort, it's just that when I have to be tested for something I have a tendency to think 'Oh no, what if I've had it all this time?'

The HIV test was an intimidating experience. Once my name was down on the clipboard we had to leave the clinic and come back at 4 p.m. for the test. We decided to go and have some more form-filling fun and went to get my drugs test. This was in another clinic, in a different part of the city. Again, the building looked like any other. It could just as well have been an office block. Inside we had to register and pay, hopping from desk to desk to desk, then queue up in a tight corridor full of people all waiting for the same thing. We stood and waited for about thirty minutes. When it came to my turn to go in to the little office people had been disappearing into, I had to put stretchy blue plastic covers on my shoes. This was the measure they took to prevent the spread of disease, however, doctors were coming and going, seemingly from lunch break to lunch break, and they never wore the blue things. Having the test involved sitting on a chair, similar to a dentist's chair, while blood was taken from my arm. The results and much needed certificate would be available a week later.

We made it back to the HIV test clinic in plenty of time. The waiting room was packed. What made it worse was that it wasn't so much of a room but a hallway at the bottom of a staircase, now used as a torture chamber for immigrants. There were at least fifty people, so many that some waited on the stairs. This annoyed nurses going back and forth. At 4 p.m. a miserable-as-fuck security guard, with huge shadows under his eyes came to the room's double doors. He locked the left one closed with a top bolt and blocked the way through on the right with his body using a wooden stand with clipboards on as a kind of barrier. At first I thought this was unusual – why a barrier? When he began calling names out, everyone else in the room got up and surged forward, pressing against the barrier and blocking the way. This pissed some of the nurses off even more when they needed to get through. It was unnecessary as everyone's names were on a list and were being read out in order. The other 'immigrants' were a bit different from me. They had dark hair and dark eyes like Nastya; most were from Azerbaijan, Kyrgyzstan or Georgia. Nastya could tell by the way that they spoke. I'm sure that most of them were nice people, looking to make a new peaceful life for themselves in Russia, yet a few of them looked seriously dangerous. They were lean, muscular, and wiry with mad staring eyes and they tended to wear thin combat-style clothing. They pushed and jostled each other like people in a bar fight. I was afraid of them, and so was Nastya who kept pulling on me slightly when one of them got too close.

The security man called out names, one by one by one, slowly. At first he shouted the names to carry over the noise made by the would-be-assassins, but he quickly tired of this and later called names in a normal voice. I think he'd been in control of would-be-assassins for too long; his patience was sorely tested. It was hard to hear my name being called out because it was said quietly and mispronounced as Meekul. When I was summoned, Nastya grabbed me and pulled me through the crowd. This was only the beginning. We had to go back to the front of the building, hand over my passport and copy of its translation for inspection, and obtain a piece of paper. We then had to get to a small booth where an old lady collected the fees and stamped the bits of paper. This paper then had to be handed over to a nurse who was taking everyone's blood. When my turn came, Nastya asked the nurse if she was using a fresh needle, which pissed her off greatly. I put on the plastic shoe covers and sat on a regular old wooden chair. She took some blood from my left arm while trading curses with Nastya, and then we were free to go. To obtain my certificate we would have to return the next day and live the same ritual all over. The following Groundhog Day we stood in the same room with the same mad-staring-eyed hard men, heard names shouted out, got jostled, queued, ferried bits of paper from one room to another, until we left with the right piece of paper – an 'I don't have Aids' certificate. My favourite certificate so far. I was well pleased because my last test had been in 2007 and I had had a few dodgy encounters with late night women since then. It also meant Nastya and I could finally have some fun without condoms, which we both hated.

After all the stress of queuing and clinics and forms and tests we took a few days off to splash about in fountains and eat ice cream. The experience of the HIV clinic had drained us and we weren't quite ready to start Round Two. Thankfully, when we were, we found that the syphilis, chlamydia and leprosy tests were all done in the same clinic and appeared on one certificate. It was a similar experience to before: indistinguishable hospital, rammed full of would-be-assassins waiting for tests and doctors/nurses walking around on permanent lunch breaks. A blood test was all that was required to be tested for syphilis and leprosy, but for the chlamydia test they wanted some piss. I had totally forgotten what STI tests were like and had already had an enjoyably long morning piss, as I do every morning, just before we left our apartment. When it came to sharing some with the nurses, I was out of piss. There were many of us queuing in the corridor, each in turn being handed a little cup to pee in, which had to be done alone in a stinky little room with a thousand-year-old toilet. When it was my turn to piss, Nastya came with me into the pee-room because she didn't like being in the corridor without me, and I think she wanted to see what the pee-room was like. The nurse, whose job it was to make sure nobody cheated, queried why Nastya and I were going into the pee-room together; she thought Nastya was the immigrant, and I was peeing in Nastya's cup to cheat the system. It was a bit embarrassing, but when she saw I couldn't speak Russian she realised I was the immigrant and let us both into the pee-room. Although I'm not at all sure why she gave Nastya permission to come in with me solely on the basis that I couldn't speak Russian. There were no instructions on the cup and, even if there were, it was quite obvious what I needed to do. This was the moment it hit me I was out of piss. Bone dry. I did my best to squeeze out a few tiny drops but it just wasn't enough. I was supposed to fill it by half at the very least, and it was a tiny cup, no bigger than a shot glass. When we exited the pee-room, I had to suffer further embarrassment because Nastya had to explain the situation and the nurse who then had to speak to another nurse, and I had to hold up my little cup with three drops of pee in it for everyone in the corridor to see. They said it might be okay, but would depend on the test. Once everyone had a cup of pee, we had to queue again at a pee-testing station: a woman with some litmus paper behind a window with iron bars. She had rubber gloves on, which was good because it was her job to dip the litmus paper into the pee cups, one by one. When it came to mine she left the paper in a while, but it was successful. I didn't have chlamydia. After going to several different offices in the same building to have my passport inspected, stamps put on papers and so on, we got the certificate. A few days later we went back to the other clinic to pick up my drugs test certificate, which said my blood was clean. This was no surprise to me. The only big task left was to fill out the temporary residency forms, but first we had to obtain them.

The centre for immigration is located on the north east of the city. It's a long bus journey from our district, and quite a difficult place to find. The district of the immigration office had taken a beating during the winter. It looked like World War III had been and gone already, with broken panels hanging off and bits missing at the bottoms of the buildings; everything has a kind of collapsed look. The ground around it is uneven to the point that cars driving past totally avoid the middle of the road, driving in a zigzag fashion. Inside the immigration centre there is a large waiting room with a number of private interview booths on one side. We made several trips to this place at the end of June. Once to obtain the residency forms, another to query sections of the forms, and again to hand all the documents in. We were told during our first visit there that once we had everything ready we had to make an appointment by phone and appointments can only be made at the end of a month for the beginning of the month following. In the last week of June Nastya was so frustrated at never being able to get through on the phone that she sent them a complaint fax from her office, saying their service was shit and that they should be ashamed of themselves. It worked. We were given an appointment in the first week of July.

On the day of the appointment our bus failed to show on time. Traffic was building up, which is unusual in the middle of the day and so when our bus came, we didn't get anywhere in a hurry. We made it as far as the west of the city centre, and got off the bus near Revolution Square with a giant statue of Lenin. Traffic was at a standstill. Our best bet was to run across to the eastern side and get a taxi. This took thirty minutes, leaving us only forty minutes before my appointment. We asked many taxis what their fare would be, and many of them took advantage of the situation by quoting 500 roubles for a 250-rouble journey; all taxis in Krasnoyarsk operate on a fixed fare basis. Finally, we found one who would drive us at a decent rate. When we told the driver our destination and explained that we were late, he put his foot down; he had also immigrated to Russia earlier in the year and appreciated how hard it was to get an appointment at the immigration office. We got there ten minutes early.

When our time came, and we stood inside the booth, the official locked the door after us using a switch underneath her desk. This was essential, as there were at least thirty other people waiting, some with just small queries, who pulled at the door in frustration. We laid out our forms, certificates and photographs and the official went through a checklist in a very matter-of-fact way. We didn't get very far down the checklist as there was a problem with my certificate of no criminal record, in that it was the wrong one. I had had a funny feeling about this certificate before I had left the UK. When I sent it to the foreign office to obtain an Apostille, it had been refused because it was issued by a 'foreign government organisation'. The certificate did say I did not have any criminal record, both in English and Russian, however it did not state in which country. It referred to any possible criminal record in Russia, not Britain. I had the wrong bloody certificate. We were told that my application for residency could not be accepted and we had to leave. Nastya burst into tears and pleaded with the official, who demonstrated that she did after all have a heart, and a smile. We were told that if we went back to their website, we could apply online and our application would be registered from that day. After five months, if my application was successful we could use all the certificates we had struggled so hard to obtain except the HIV certificate. In the meantime, I was told I could obtain the correct criminal records certificate during those five months and return at wintertime on another private visa.

We went home shattered and slightly demoralised. Nastya filled in the form online and submitted it; this took several attempts as my photograph needed to be scanned and attached to the form with the focus perfect and lighting just so. In addition, the photograph we had taken by a professional photographer had a light blue background, and it needed to be grey. It was all very annoying and Nastya cursed a tremendous amount. Meanwhile I contacted the British embassy in Moscow who replied the next day. The certificate I needed had to be obtained from my local police station in Cardiff and would be issued forty days exactly after I paid £10 and made an official request. Both those trips to London had been unnecessary. It was the first and only mistake I made with regard to visas and immigration stuff. Not bad really, considering how many Hula-Hoops I had to jump through.

151

Propaganda

Sitting in the new apartment I felt relief at being able to stay in one place for three months. When in the UK I usually had to travel a lot for work; not only that, but I had rented rooms since the age of twenty and had to leave the house I had been living in for five years after I left my bank job in 2007. Since then, and before meeting Nastya, I had spent years trying to make my way in the world of literature while sleeping here there and everywhere. I didn't make the transition to my parents' houses immediately, at first I sofa-surfed. In one year I slept in over two hundred different places, including one night on a large inflatable crocodillo. Many see the life of a poet as debauched, full of women, drink and dossing around for the fun of it. In reality, a poet's life is full of study with the constant worry of where to spend the night. Drink just eases the destitution a fraction. Now we had an apartment of our own, a bed, walls, a door, and a new fridge – I had never had a new fridge before – the sensation of beginning a fresh life was exaggerated because everything was shiny. We had to buy forks and spoons and things like measuring jugs. We only had two plates; we needed more. It had taken many years of trying different careers, travelling around, sleeping in odd places, and a few failed relationships, but looking around at our very own place of tranquillity I could see that life was finally shaping out just like I wished it.

As Nastya was the breadwinner, I took it upon myself to clean the apartment and do the cooking. Vacuum cleaners do exist in Russia, although I have never seen one, or know of anybody who has one. Instead, Russians use a broomstick, like the type that witches are supposed to fly about on, but with a slightly shorter handle. When Nastya was in work I would sweep away, and then do the mopping. I became a perfectly house-proud househusband. Washing machines in Russia are also a bit different. They look like normal machines front-on but they are not very deep. This is because there simply isn't the room in most Russian apartments to house a full-size machine. It is a waste of space. Washing machines can be anything from 8,000 roubles (about £160); we didn't have that sort of money lying spare so I carried our washing to Nastya's parents' apartment and used theirs every two weeks or as needed. When we only had a few small things to wash like pants and socks, I did them in the bath by hand. At first I was pissed off by the situation – because I had grown up in a world of washing machines – but it also served as a reminder about my childhood. When I was a boy we had had a humungous machine that took up half the kitchen, and when it died my dad put it in the back garden to rot. It wasn't completely useless as it turned out to be the perfect place for my sisters and I to store our Plaster of Paris sculptures of soldiers we made from a kit we had been given by an aunt. We never painted them, and so when the machine was later taken by the council to the scrapyard it had in its drum a ball of white powdery soldiers, bound together by fungus. During that time my mum had to wash the clothes in the bath. I must have been about five or six but I remember with absolute clarity how hard she worked. Her hands were red, blistered, and cold to the touch because the hot water was too expensive to use. Rinsing my pants in unlimited hot water, I thought of her and all the pains she had gone through to raise four kids. It was hard enough for me just to wash the clothes of two, let alone a family of six.

Sometimes, when I didn't want to visit Nastya's parents or wash clothes in the bath, I was given a helping hand by one of our neighbours. Directly across from our apartment, on the eastern side of the building lives Benya, an old school friend of Nastya's. She lent us many things over the summer and let us use her washing machine from time to time. As a thank you for her help, we often invited her to our apartment for weekend drinks. For some reason we were never invited to her apartment. It was clear that Benya obsessed over her body and self-image, to the point of looking like Lolo Ferrari, but Nastya suspected she took less care of her apartment, which was rumoured to look like a cross between a Barbie house and an overflowing skip. Even so, with Benya's generosity we were able to get by quite easily until we could afford all the kitchen utensils and furniture we needed, and her constant pouting also provided us with hours of entertainment on weekends.

It was a tremendously hot summer, much worse than 2011. The temperature rose to 38 °C in June and lingered around that point until mid-August. If we had lived with Nastya's parents I would have walked around in what is known as a home-shirt. This is a very Russian thing; it's a standard length, thick, checkered shirt that is made of a cheap material so it's okay to get it dirty. It was so hot that I couldn't bother with my home-shirt at all; I didn't bother with any shirt for that matter. In the privacy of our own home Nastya and I walked around in our birthday suits. This was still too many clothes. Sat at the kitchen table, which fast became my favourite place to write, a pool of sweat would appear at my feet and fill my home shoes. This perspiration was constant, even if I didn't wear anything. To cool off we would both take cold showers every hour, without bothering to dry ourselves as we would be soaking again within five minutes anyway. Our balcony became our cooling-off place. After cold showers we would stand for a few minutes on the balcony with the blinds completely closed and the windows open all the way. The balcony windows are very tall and are of the sliding frame variety, fully open they let in a lovely cool breeze; at night-time, we occasionally put a mattress down on the balcony floor and slept there, even though we were eaten by mosquitoes.

Other than Benya, we didn't get to know our other neighbours very well. We did however get to learn a bit about our neighbour in the apartment above us. Almost every night he played loud trance music and had people over who would dance until 3 a.m. It was worst on weekends, there were more people and we would sometimes see them hanging out of the balcony window above us, smoking cigarettes and dribbling mucus. We determined that our music-loving neighbour was in his early twenties. Although we never knew his name, due to his late night partying he came to be known as 'that bastard'. At around 3 to 4 a.m. his parties would end and it quietened down enough to get some decent sleep. This affected Nastya more than it did me, as I wasn't working and I've had insomnia since 2005. Also I grew up in Ely, where late-night parties on any night are the norm.

I know how important it is for a young man to look after and nurture his 'man-image'; young men always do their utmost to dress well and must be seen to listen to the most popular tunes of the time, though everyone has their secret guilty pleasures. When I was sixteen and listening to the likes of the Manics and Joy Division, my guilty pleasure was *ABBA – The Movie*. So it came as no surprise to me when at 8:30 a.m. after the party hard-man had been asleep just a few hours, I would be woken by his alarm; in place of a normal ringing sound or the radio coming on, I was woken by Bucks Fizz 'The Land of Make Believe' at full volume. It's amazing what guilty pop pleasures some people have, most but not all of which are entirely forgivable.

On days when Nastya was working, after I had cleaned the apartment I could either sit in the kitchen and write or lean out the balcony window and watch the world go by. I could have left the apartment if I'd wanted to, and I did want to, but I was still afraid. Not knowing the language crippled me. Plus I was intimidated by the streets and the people who walked along them. It wasn't like Paris where I could scrape by on the pigeon French I had been forced to learn in high school. In Russia I had no means of communication and the architecture, the pavements, even the birds of prey circling outside the balcony helped cement my view that I was in a hostile country. If I stepped out of the front door and locked it behind me, I couldn't guarantee my safe return.

Across from our building was a small scrap of grass, partly covered in litter and dog shit. Over the summer I watched as a babushka came out of her apartment, cleaned the area, dug the ground, fenced it off and planted a small herb garden. She came out every day in the early morning and late afternoon to water her plants. Her little garden was never vandalised, the young people seemed to have an ingrained sense of respect for the babushkas and the efforts they made. It wasn't just one little garden opposite us, everywhere in Krasnoyarsk I saw the elderly tidying the areas outside their dilapidated apartment buildings. They made a great effort and it made an astonishing difference to the suburban areas of the city. Whether in summer or winter, the most common sight in Krasnoyarsk is seeing the many babushkas walking around with food shopping. My mother-in-law is one of them. She may be in her sixties but the rule is that anyone with grandchildren, regardless of age, is a babushka. Though Nataliya Petrovna once broke her neck in a serious accident that almost killed her when she was younger, she still managed to accomplish everything she needed to and more. She looked after Semka during weekdays and some weekends, took him to school, took him to his karate class, took him shopping – there was nothing that was too much for her. During the summer months she always helps Boris plant the crops at the dacha and waters them every day. At the apartment she has to climb the four flights of concrete stairs many times a day. She shifts furniture, barrels of water, logs for the fire, anything. To look at the way she moves and the way she lives, she puts Nastya and me to shame. It may sound strange and probably a bit patronising for me to praise her this way, because she is after all only in her sixties, and this is still quite a young age, but there is a huge difference between pensioners in Siberia and pensioners in Britain. By retirement age a Siberian has not only lived through sixty winters, but sixty Siberian winters. The weather, the painful and life-threatening cold takes its toll on people's bodies, to the point that I would say a Siberian winter is worth two or three British winters. Compared with my grandparents in the UK, Nataliya Petrovna is a superwoman, though in Russia she is no different from the millions of other babushkas. When I see them doing their daily shopping, with hunched backs and short legs, they look like small armoured vehicles. There is no weight that is too much, no distance too far, and no weather system too harsh; babushkas are the backbone of Russia, and without them the country would come to a standstill.

Something else I noticed during the summer was the repair of the roads. In my poem 'There are no problems in Russia' I state that there are many roads with potholes that drivers need to swerve constantly in order to avoid. This is true but not all year round. The winter ice is often several inches if not several feet thick, and this ice lifts paving slabs, wreaking havoc with flat surfaces. In the summer of 2012, I witnessed a major effort to replace thousands of paving and kerb stones. A small army of construction workers laboured away all summer laying new paving and filling the potholes created by the winter ice. I was wrong to give the impression that the roads in Russia are broken and the problem ignored. Seeing the huge workforce made me realise what an unimaginably expensive affair it must be to keep the roads in constant good repair. Russia is big enough to swallow central Europe several times over, it's hard to conceive how many roads there are, the quantity of materials needed and the manpower required to keep it all working smoothly. Another line in my poem insinuates the militia is corrupt and only ever intervenes in crimes where it can squeeze a bribe out of someone. I have never seen this in real life. I have actually enjoyed a slice of cake and a cup of coffee in a café while sat at a table next to some militia on their lunch break. They did not ask to see my papers even though I was clearly speaking English. Similarly I have never been harassed or stopped in the street, though I stand out like an amateur among poets. Shamefully I have to admit that this poem is largely influenced by anti-Russian propaganda, and a few articles in newspapers, and as time passes a lot of my early beliefs and impressions have been altered by my own Siberian experiences.

Line of Sight

In the middle of July, on one of the hottest days, Nastya took me to a place called Orbit; this is a concrete platform near a branch of the Siberian Federal University, on the north west side of the riverbank. It's quite high above sea level and offers a view of riverside dachas below as well as the city centre to the east. It's a favourite place for lovers to go in summer because of its remoteness. There is also the best view of Krasnoyarsk Railway Bridge anywhere in the city; this bridge is famous for carrying part of the Trans-Siberian Railway across the Yenisei. It is one of the most romantic bridges in the world and I was glad to see it from such a great viewpoint. Near Orbit is a small suburban area named Akademgorodok, or the Academia City. It's not so much a city, more a little cul-de-sac where the students live in relatively smart looking apartments. A few hundred metres west of this is another suburban area with twenty or so buildings. These are some of the poorest looking apartments in the city and a stark contrast to the student buildings.

As we walked high above the Yenisei, we noticed a lot of construction sites and cranes on either side of the river. Many swanky-looking apartment buildings were going up fast. The whole riverbank area seemed to be going through an overdue period of reconstruction; some of the apartments looked so attractive they could have been built along the Thames. When it was time to leave, we walked inland and found ourselves at the eastern end of the street where the bus had dropped us off. We couldn't make out exactly where the bus stop was as the signposts were missing. There were one or two couples walking so Nastya asked them for directions. They shied away. This is normal in Russia where the Soviet years forced a culture of suspicion. No matter which part of the city we ask directions, people have always walked away from us, pretending they didn't hear or just brazenly ignoring us. This time it was obvious we weren't thieves, Soviet spies or KGB informers as Nastya said out loud 'We are lost, please just point to the bus stop.' One of the couples gave in and told us where to stand. At the bus stop Nastya began to shout 'Get your back to a tree, you could be shot.' I adjusted my position to not leave any part of my body visible to anyone in the apartment windows behind us. Nastya said that in poorer areas of Krasnoyarsk there are some people who live on dubious incomes. In these areas some people carry guns and will shoot at someone in their area simply for being stupid enough to leave themselves open. I put my back to a tree and waited for the bus.

As it was my fourth time in Siberia, and my spoken Russian was improving, I steadily felt less afraid walking around on my own. I started walking Nastya to the bus stop when she was leaving for her night shift at 7.30 p.m. and would then walk home alone. When she came to the end of a day shift, I would leave our apartment at 7.20 p.m. and walk to her office along populated main roads. This had begun as a very pleasant thing to do. However, with the possible-sniper experience of Akademgorodok, the pleasure of walking around on my own diminished somewhat; I began to walk faster and became very suspicious of people within a close proximity to me. This was of course totally irrational as nobody meant me any harm. When I walk anywhere I usually have a song on repeat in my head. I have songs for different occasions, and different memories. Up until that time the soundtrack accompaniment to my walk to Nastya's office had been Bowie's 'Golden Years'; but this unfortunately changed to the main theme of John Carpenter's 1976 ~~movie~~ *film* *Assault on Precinct 13*. As I walked down the street, I heard the initial 'Rat-a-tat-a-tat. Rat-a-tat-a-tat' before 'Du-du-du-du-dun'. I had visions of cars packed with badasses cruising past with semi-automatics complete with silencers. God forbid I walk past an ice cream van.

What is Good for a Welshman is Great for a Siberian

There's an old joke that goes something like this: An Englishman, a Frenchman and a Russian are admiring a painting of Adam and Eve. The Englishman says 'Look at the paleness of Eve's skin, the rose-red of her cheeks; she must be English.' The Frenchman says 'Look at the way they are looking deep into each other's eyes, they are full of romance, and must be French.' The Russian finally adds 'They have no clothes and only an apple to eat, and they think it's paradise. They are Russian.' Ignoring the fact that this will be extremely offensive to many people, there is an element of truth in the way it stereotypes Russian people.

The Soviet government famously attempted to instil in its population a belief that Russia was some kind of utopia; but had a lot of trouble doing so while Stalin's government went round killing millions of people. Even so, there are inordinate numbers of Russian people I have met who believe that Russia is practically faultless. While initially I may have had some of my facts wrong as a result of Western anti-Russian propaganda, there are several factors of Russian life that are indisputably unfair and in some cases dangerous; for example: when the roads and pavements were repaired over the summer there were no barriers preventing people from hurting themselves. Twice I was nearly killed by walking into a reversing JCB or mini-crane. The kerbstones, which were dug up initially by heavy machinery, were left alongside the road jutting out in all directions. Cars had to be careful to avoid them and crossing the road meant stepping into the ditch where previous kerbing was, hopping through the myriad of rubble, climbing over the old kerbstones and then doing the same on the opposite side. For the elderly and disabled it was practically impossible in some places. When buildings and railings are removed, they are simply cut off with a grinder about 10 cm from the ground; this leaves metal poles sticking up everywhere. While one could argue it simply takes common sense to avoid these dangers it made me very grateful for the often all too easily criticised health and safety laws back in the UK. Besides building-related issues, food safety standards in Russia are clearly ignored. None of the eggs in our fridge were ever in date, and with the regular power outages it was hard to say just how many times everything in the freezer had defrosted and refrozen. Cheese in Russia is arguably the same stuff that bouncy balls are made from and most milk products are laced with palm oil.

Although my life in Russia is generally a vast improvement on my life in the UK, I can't avoid the fact that I have been spoilt in some ways by Western standards and cultural differences. Before visiting Siberia, I had never had to show my passport to board a train, never had to fetch water from a well or grow my own food. I have never in my life had to rely on someone's ability to hunt for deer to avoid starvation, and I have never had to work any period in any job for free, even when the economy was at its worst. Life in the West isn't perfect; certainly there are faults in the capitalist system, and the current British government are doing their very best to make life harder for the working classes, but it's easier in many ways compared with life in the East.

As a Westerner, I am spoilt. I have come to expect everything to be available in the supermarket; I expect everything to be within date; for buildings and roads to be repaired in a timely fashion; and for hospitals to have the latest technologies and to have access to modern medicine instantly, thanks to the NHS. I would have said that I expect the public transport to be of a certain standard and to provide seating, but the fact is that the train service in Russia is a vast improvement on the service provided by Arriva Trains Wales. These standards that I am accustomed to as a Westerner have often amazed my Siberian family, and although Siberians have the luxury of dacha lifestyles and a wide-open country to explore, what is considered 'good' by Western standards is 'great' from the Siberian perspective. This newfound insight hasn't made the transition to Russian life any easier for me. There have been occasions in supermarkets when I just wanted to grab the owner by the scruff of the neck and shout 'Why can't you provide stock that is in date!' Similarly, I have wanted to knock some sense into friends of mine in the UK who have spent time feeling sorry for themselves. There was once an occasion when a friend of mine was forced to cancel their satellite television subscription because of the recession. When this cancellation was then posted on Facebook, my friend received several messages of condolence and sympathy. Apparently, such a loss was considered really awful. To top it off this friend then went on to say how he was considering moving to Russia to escape the UK austerity measures. He wasn't joking. One of my worst memories is of Moscow, when I saw a 90-year-old homeless babushka next to a metro station begging for food. It's an image that will never leave me. Thousands, if not hundreds of thousands of babushkas suffered the awfulness of being forced to beg on the streets following the collapse of the USSR. I wanted to grab my Satellite-TV-less friend in the UK and implant my memory of the homeless babushka; but I couldn't. It's not for me to judge others' perception of value, although I sometimes find this hard.

As much as I hate to admit it, I too was once this ignorant, though I have only glimpsed a fraction of the suffering of those who have lived through Russia's several economic crashes. There are some who would look at me and say 'He knows nothing of real hardship and his new-found insight and perception of value is contrived and middle-class.' And they might be right; I have not seen people living on $1 a day, or witnessed the slavery in Chinese factories; but I have seen enough to help me realise that I am a spoilt bastard and was lucky to be born in Wales. Saying this I don't want to appear to sympathise with British Conservative values. I do not subscribe to the notion that British people don't know how good they have it, and therefore can afford to lose most of their libraries, their affordable education system and large chunks of the NHS. These things have been hard earned and should be preserved at all costs. Just because life in Britain is for the most part far easier than life in Post-Soviet countries, it doesn't mean we shouldn't strive to improve it further. Seeing something as essential as the NHS being sold off bit-by-bit hurts even more, watching from a distance.

Siberian life has given me a more in-depth appreciation of certain British values and it pains me to see the welfare state under attack, and the poor being played off against each other. I didn't realise just how fundamentally essential the welfare state and the NHS were until I saw them being dismantled from afar. When the USSR collapsed, Nastya's parents had no option other than to work for free, however such conditions seemed inevitable when you consider that the entire Eastern Bloc was undergoing its biggest social, political and economic reform since the USSR began. Although the global economic crash of 2007 was a major setback for the British economy, the resulting crisis wasn't anywhere near as extreme as the Russian crisis less than twenty years earlier. Therefore, when I read about people being forced to work for free as part of the Workfare scheme it seemed to me completely obvious that such measures were unnecessary. Knowing this, when Nataliya Petrovna said that in her opinion 'What was good for a Welshman was great for a Siberian' I had to really fight to hold my tongue.

The Uninvited

Rain in Siberia is a rare phenomenon but when it happens it's as dramatic as the winter weather. One afternoon when Nastya was home and we felt it was too hot to go out, we passed the time by hanging out of the balcony window, smoking cigarettes and drinking home-made lemonade. The sky darkened in the west, filling with oppressive clouds that stretched out for miles. When the rain began to fall it was a very welcome change to the atmosphere; the large store of water behind the hydroelectric station means that Krasnoyarsk can be very humid in the summer, making the air stuffy. We watched as people below us attempted to protect themselves, putting their shopping bags on their heads or using a t-shirt as a hat. When the first rumble of thunder shook the sky we pulled up some of the stools from the kitchen, resigning ourselves to spending the remainder of the day watching the weather.

The rain clouds enveloped all of the summer blue, stopping short of our apartment building. A series of lightning bolts struck one after the other above the apartment block across the way; not single bolts, but impressive lances of forked lightning, long and intimidating. I had only ever witnessed a similar display when I was living in Abertridwr in 2000, and it was considered so rare it made the headlines of all the newspapers the following day. The residents of the opposite block, who had been hiding from the sun, came out onto their balconies, and strained their necks to watch the lightning above them. It went on for hours, though it was such an exotic event for me that I didn't notice the day pass by.

Nastya, who enjoyed the display as much as I did, cautioned me to be ready to move back very quickly, and asked me to close the window up to the point where the sash nearly met the frame. She wanted to continue watching the storm through the glass. She was worried lightning would come into our apartment and cook us where we sat. Thinking she was bonkers I told her the satellite dishes, antennae and air conditioning systems on the roofs would likely connect to the forks of electricity way before lightning bolts reached down, bent horizontally and zapped us. I was wrong. In Russia there exists a phenomenon known as ball lightning. This is an unexplained electrical phenomenon that refers to white spheres that appear to float down from the sky. Unlike forked lightning these balls of electricity have the ability to move horizontally. They are usually associated with thunderstorms, but can last considerably longer than the split-second flash of a regular lightning bolt. It is said that these balls eventually explode like grenades and can be fatal if they connect to you or if you unlucky enough to be too close during the explosion. Although there are many theories concerning nature's electronic balls of death no one really knows for sure why they happen.

Nastya would often ring me from her night shift after she'd received a call from her mother at the dacha. As we lived so close to their apartment, I was often nominated to go there and give Baba Ira her heart pills so that Boris didn't have to drive back. I'd normally get a call by 10 p.m., not so late that I would be sleeping but late enough for me to see it would be totally unreasonable for anyone else to do it. Not that it was any great hardship walking for five minutes up the street. In the middle of summer the sun doesn't set until about midnight, sometimes later. The pink sky of dusk can still be seen on the horizon until it becomes the pink sky of dawn. Pitch blackness is rare and only occurs if there is cloud cover. When I entered the other apartment, searched out the pills that would normally be stored in an old biscuit tin in Nastya's old bedroom, and handed them over, I often wondered whether I should stick around. I felt sad for Ira's lonely existence. With hindsight I see that this was merely sentimentality on my behalf. Ira, like anyone, probably enjoyed having the apartment all to herself. She would play the radio, spend time in the kitchen and call her friends on the phone. There was no noise, no Semka running about, no bickering between Boris and Nataliya Petrovna over where he had placed his hunting bags, and no obstacles to negotiate while shuffling from room to room on her support stool. Although we couldn't communicate with each other very well, we always did our best to exchange kind words and always spoke in the most respectful tones. Baba Ira survived eighty-nine years in Siberia, eighty-nine winters, eighty-nine scorching summers; she lost her sons, her husband, and her father (who disappeared during Stalin's purges), but she still managed to get up every day. She dressed very well regardless of occasion and managed to keep regular hours of sleep and wakefulness, something that I have never been able to do; if I have more than one week without work I usually end up staying awake till 3 a.m. or worse. With little else to do, those regular visits to Ira gave me some sense of purpose and responsibility.

As Nastya was stuck in her office whole nights and I'd now spent three months without work, my sleeping pattern became erratic. I would stay up all night when I was alone, and sleep in the day with Nastya when she returned at 9 a.m. Those were strange nights. Usually after eating, washing, doing the dishes and sweeping the floor with the broomstick, I settled down at the kitchen table to write. I sat in the corner next to the radiator, as far from the fridge as possible, because if I sat close to the fridge I would be visible to the residents in the opposite block. We started leaving the blinds open when the balcony windows were open, because if the blinds were shut they would rattle in the wind and be loud enough to annoy our neighbours and alert the world that our apartment was wide open. Between midnight and sunrise I wrote by the light of my laptop, keeping the lamp off so as not to be seen. I became quite paranoid during those nights. I think this had a lot to do with total isolation, having only Nastya to speak to online, and the continuous explosions coming from the nearby electricity sub-station, which made me feel that I was alive in some Solzhenitsyn novel where the KGB bugged all the rooms and had fake neighbours positioned in the apartments with a view of ours. When I wanted to make tea, I would walk very slowly over to the counter even though it was only a few feet away, because the floor boards would creak when I stepped on them.

I didn't want to make a sound at night, and I didn't want to be seen either. Sat in the darkness I often had the feeling of being watched. I suspected other nocturnal people existed in the opposite building. Sometimes I could see a shadow moving on one of the balconies; sometimes a cigarette would be lit. I was always careful to light my cigarette with my hands covering the lighter, but it was no use, I could always be seen no matter how careful I was. When I saw someone stood in the darkness on their balcony, often staring, watching for any movement, I had the distinct impression that they were watching me; I could feel their eyes on me. Regardless of how careful I was, I couldn't blend into the darkness as well as my Siberian neighbours. They were experts. I might as well have turned on all the lights and worn sparkly clothes because I was about as good at discretion as a blazing bonfire. This ability to see without being seen is a skill I assume most people learned during the Soviet years. Everyone was naturally suspicious of everyone else; your neighbour could be an informer, or worse, your neighbour could be KGB. Why were you awake so late? Were you writing? What were you writing? I had seen for myself how people still shy away from each other in the street; that fear of saying the wrong thing or speaking to the wrong person still exists. It is safer not to speak, not to write, but if you do have to write, as I do, it's important to learn how to be a shadow. You never know who is watching.

There would sometimes be a ring at the door when I was home alone. When the bell rung, I froze; very few people answer the door to strangers, or even the militia, choosing instead to communicate through closed doors. With my limited Russian I couldn't even do that. Instead I turned off any music and pretended I wasn't there. I couldn't open the peep-hole at the centre of the door as it would have let light out and made it obvious I was there, plus the fact that our floor creaks like hell. If the bell rang before midnight it was sometimes Benya who had run out of sugar or coffee; though she normally phoned Nastya who would then call me from her office. Sometimes the bell rang in the early hours, while I was writing or sleeping. We had bought the apartment from a middle-aged single mum with a teenage son; logic dictated some of the daytime calls were possibly his friends or family members who didn't know they had moved. The night-time calls could not be explained. Despite our steel-plated front door, every time the bell rang it scared the hell out of me as I also knew that there are keys available on the black market that are specifically designed for opening Russian doors; they have several malleable segments at the tip and make armoured doors as useful as paper shutters. Though someone with such a key probably wouldn't have rung the bell if they'd wanted to get in. Those late night calls were likely caused by a drunken neighbour pressing the wrong button outside the door at the end of the corridor, but it was impossible to know at the time. The fact was we lived in a decrepit old building and had some very dubious looking neighbours; when I took the lift in the morning to get cigarettes, there were occasional pools of blood on the floor mixed with other human juices. Although I really loved our new apartment, and having time alone to write, those solitary nights were some of the most terrifying I've ever had.

Krasnoyarsk 26, the Secret City

Not all of my time alone during those all-nighters was spent writing. Much time was also spent pissing about on the internet, talking to Nastya on Facebook Chat and looking up odd facts about Russia, in between tiptoeing to the kitchen to make tea.

While looking into the history of Krasnoyarsk, I kept coming across the phrase 'Krasnoyarsk nuclear contamination'. I found dozens of articles giving sketchy details of Krasnoyarsk's nuclear facilities and an apparent environmental disaster. In my sleep-deprived state of delirium, reading reports of contamination, radiation sicknesses and pollution of the Yenisei, my heart raced with caffeinated panic at the thought that I might be living in a nuclear-contaminated city. While some articles referred to Krasnoyarsk, others referred to Krasnoyarsk 26 (K26) and Krasnoyarsk 45 (K45). I typed these names into Google maps hoping to distinguish one from the other. I had no such luck; the map led straight to the centre of Krasnoyarsk city. This is because K26 and K45 were no longer known by these names, but were now Zheleznogorsk and Zelenogorsk respectively. With further research I discovered that K26 and K45 were 'secret cities', created during the cold war to produce weapons-grade plutonium and enriched uranium. The reason I couldn't find them on the map was that under the Soviet Union, secret cities were given names of PO Boxes inside well-established cities. K45 is the number of a post office located in Krasnoyarsk, while K26, I am told, is a PO Box number that probably refers to a village just a few miles out from Krasnoyarsk city.

Since the collapse of the USSR, the existence of forty-two secret cities, now known as closed cities, has been disclosed to the public, while there are rumours that at least another fifteen or more have not yet been revealed. Until 1992 these closed cities didn't exist on any maps. There were no road signs to or from them and their names didn't appear on train timetables. To gain access people were subject to document checks and were required to obtain special permission from the KGB. Closed cities were often protected by a perimeter fence, barbed wire and security checkpoints. Although they looked like giant prison camps, the residents, of which there were normally more than fifty thousand per city, were able to come and go, as long as they didn't give any reference to where they had come from. Their very homes were deemed 'classified information'. K26 was established in 1950 for the production of plutonium. Also known as 'Atom Town' and the 'Iron City', much of K26 was built underground at huge expense to protect it from nuclear attack. Defence complexes including nuclear fuel production reactors, bomb production and radioactive waste removal plants were built within caverns inside the granite mountain on the northern edge of the city. This was an ideal place as compared with most other types of rock, granite has been known to contain a higher amount of naturally occurring radioactive elements such as radium, uranium and thorium, which meant any foreign technology with the ability to detect radioactive particles would overlook this site.

Throughout my late night investigation into K26, I was confused by many of the articles I read including a BBC article from 1998 which came complete with a map of Russia with a little radiation sign over Krasnoyarsk; this is because some articles referred to Krasnoyarsk, when in fact they were discussing facilities at K26 and K45. Occasionally articles mentioned Krasnoyarsk when they were referring to the entire region rather than the city. This inaccurate information led to me working myself into a state the following day; I decided to conduct my own tests. I emailed many of my friends in the UK who I knew to have careers in science or who worked for a university and could therefore approach someone who knew about radiation and nuclear contamination. I also needed a Geiger counter. Boris, who has hunted all over Siberia has a Geiger counter that he uses to ensure the ground he hunts on, the berries he picks and the deer he catches aren't radioactive. After a quick word with Nastya, Boris came over to our flat the morning following my night of research. With his help, we tested all the food in the fridge, the water, every room of the apartment and nearly every household object. It turned out that the most radioactive item was the laptop I had brought with me from the UK. Panic over. However, Boris did explain to me through Nastya that while most things in Krasnoyarsk were safe, there were items sold in shops that were contaminated with radiation from K26, as well as areas in Krasnoyarsk south of the river that while not entirely radioactive, were contaminated through pollution from the metal factories. From that day on, we were very careful about what we bought in the supermarkets, questioning the origin of each product. Some shop staff were surprised and even smirked when we told them we didn't want chicken from cities known to be radioactive. They were either totally unaware such food contamination existed or were amused by our concern, because they believed the notion of radioactive chicken was far-fetched.

While I continued researching the nuclear industry in Russia, I was horrified to learn of several disasters that are little known to the West, some of which resulted in contamination and nuclear fallout similar in scale to that of the Chernobyl disaster. The Mayak nuclear complex located near the city of Chelyabinsk has been described as 'the most polluted place on Earth'. Besides many accounts of 'death and disease' and the evacuation of nearly twenty villages as a result of nuclear waste being dumped into the Techa River nearby, a hushed up explosion of a nuclear waste storage tank in 1957 released radiation equal to 'more than half the amount of radioactive waste released by the accident in

Chernobyl'. Similar reports of pollution can also be read about other nuclear facilities such as Tomsk-7. With scant information being released from what the Soviets called 'closed reports' and the results of the most detailed investigations deemed 'classified', I could see why some media outlets were often confused about which city was which. Over a period of weeks I managed to piece together likely facts after cross-referencing many reports found because of lengthy online searches. These documents included reports on nuclear and environmental disasters not only in Russia but elsewhere in the world, including the UK and the now famous Fukushima. What became apparent was the culture of secrecy and cover-ups wasn't unique to Russian or Soviet culture, but was and is widespread throughout the rest of the world; I concluded my investigation with the knowledge that every country has its dirty secrets that none of us will ever fully realise and that I would be better off not trawling the internet when I should be sleeping.

Dachnik

When I lived in Pentyrch back in 2003, I did all of my drinking in the Lewis Arms at the top of the hill. I preferred it to the Kings Arms at the bottom, because I didn't like walking back up to the top of the village after a skinful, and the Lewis Arms had a round pool table that was shit to play on but tons of fun when pissed. One evening, about 10.30 p.m., two blokes walked in with uncommon accents. They were from North Wales. They sat on the stools closest to the bar on the front side of the building and ordered two pints. Jeff, being your normal curious landlord asked them where they were from and what their business was in Pentyrch. I don't remember where they said they came from, what mattered is that after only one pint they went on to call us English. This is due to the irrational view shared by only a handful of Welsh people that those from the north are somehow Welshier than folk from the south. After that the conversation became quite heated and the two travellers departed without finishing their drinks. This kind of banter also exists in Russia, except it's more of an east/west thing. Russians in the west of the Urals are seen as Euro-Russians while those in the east are seen simply as Russian or Siberian-Russian. Siberians, unlike their Western cousins, tend to hold themselves in higher regard because they live through more extreme weather conditions and a far harsher economic climate; and most of the bears and other man-eating beasts are in Siberia. It's less developed than the west, particularly Moscow, so it's seen as Old Russia, the original land with the original people. Siberians are also credited with winning the Battle of Stalingrad, which of course is the battle that turned the tide of World War II. When choosing men to go and fight on the front line it is claimed the Soviet Marshal Chuikov said to the new soldiers: 'Step forward if you are from Siberia. To defend Stalingrad I need men who know how to put all they can into a fight; others get back to positions behind Volga.' Chuikov later went on to say 'Siberians were the soul of the Stalingrad battle.' Siberians are famously strong, and they understand that Moscow is nothing without them; they live in the main body of Russia, and consequently they sit on top of Russia's vast mineral reserves. They are a stoic people, with all the strength and cunning of the bears they live alongside. Before I came to Russia, I could only have spoken to you of Moscow, because that's the only city I'd heard much about; my knowledge of the land beyond the Urals was shameful. What I know now is that Siberia is also Russia and Moscow; Putin and the Kremlin are powerless without its support.

What I love most about living in Siberia is that we are reminded that we are not in charge; nature is the ruling power. There are a host of bears, wild dogs and cats that are large, ferocious and love to eat meat and yet Siberians live alongside these creatures. Humans are not the dominant force, like everything else we are part of the food chain; lower your guard for long enough in Siberia and something will come along with its big teeth and paws and remind you of this fact. As a result there exists a greater respect for other creatures; humans live in the towns and cities, but the taiga is shared with all manner of birds and beasts. They have their playground and we have ours. In my view this co-existence with man-eating beasts gives Siberians a greater sense of humility. When I was a boy, growing up in the West, I was taught that man is the greatest, most evolved species on Earth; that all other beasts big or small are subservient to his power. Now I know otherwise.

During each of my previous visits to Russia, Boris had asked me if I would like to accompany him to his hut in the mountains to learn how to hunt. I declined every time because I'm not brave enough. This was fine with Boris and Nataliya Petrovna, but they insisted that I still had to learn at least some of their ways over the summer. I was, after all, a new addition to the family, another mouth to feed, and so needed to contribute something. Marina and Boris took it upon themselves to teach me how to grow vegetables; firstly by showing me how to plough the land and remove any weeds; and secondly how to plant each vegetable and water each one differently. In reality Boris and Marina did most of the work throughout the summer, with only occasional help from me, because Nastya and I only visited the dacha for short periods in between Nastya's work shifts; however all the squash were entirely my effort. By the end of July we had quite a large crop of nearly everything required to take the family right through to winter. When we were at our apartment Boris often drove over with bags of vegetables to save us from having to lug them home on the bus, and he usually included a few extras, like milk or bread, just to keep us going. The fridge in our apartment was stuffed with various homegrown goods, while various other root vegetables were placed in our family's underground storage box to keep them cool and safe. Many Siberians have one of these storage boxes. They can be seen all over the city. What look like little wooden platforms with padlocks on just a few inches from the ground in between apartment blocks are in fact people's vegetable stores. They are actually steel boxes that go several feet underground and are the perfect way to keep vegetables because they keep vegetables cool and fresh all year.

Outside our apartment there is an old chest of drawers that has long been abandoned. Inside there is a variety of junk, including old calendars. When Boris visited he normally had a rummage around in the chest to see if there was anything of value. He took one of the calendars home as the paper was quite thick and could be used to wrap food in his hunting kit. Nastya told me that Boris once salvaged a pile of left over material and animal fur from the rubbish dump outside his apartment, which pleased Nataliya Petrovna no end. Boris didn't care; he washed the material several times and after a period of weeks had fashioned himself a very smart fur waistcoat. At the dacha I watched as he took an old square piece of wood that I thought was junk, and made a new seat for the boat he uses to go hunting. He spent hours every evening with the wood on his lap, carving away with his chisels until he had a seat with intricate carving that looked professionally made. It just goes to show that one Western man's rubbish is another Siberian man's hunting accessory.

When I wasn't learning the art of growing veg or ploughing the land in summer, Nastya and I would walk through the forest in between rows of old dachas to get to one of the nearby lakes. Sometimes we would go for a swim but more often than not we would just sit and watch the world go by. Seeing the perfectly sculpted bodies of the young men in the lake made me too self-conscious to get my kit off and reveal my well-fed poet's physique. To get to our favourite lake we walked along a path that led halfway to Pugachevo train station. This route was littered with giant concrete blocks with old twisted steel spikes protruding at all angles. No one could explain why they were there. I assumed they were once protection or housing for the many rusting fuel tanks found littering Pugachevo. These beasts are ex-cargo railway wagons, roughly 50 ft long and at least 20 ft high; I assumed that before Pugachevo was a dacha territory it must have had another purpose, unless those tanks were used for water before the wells were dug and the piping laid from the lakes to the dachas.

There are many Soviet ruins throughout Krasnoyarsk and the neighbouring dacha territories that are all gradually eroding; disused factories are crumbling to the ground, leaving twisted steel bars reaching out from the rubble like the fingers of some terrible machine buried alive. Any parts of the Soviet machine that are of use have been salvaged: factory walls and roofs have become dacha walls and vegetable dividers. It's as if Russia is a giant recycling plant, only in the process of separating the useful from the rubbish its task is to reconstruct itself at the same time.

When we were tired of the lake we sometimes walked the twenty-minute path to Pugachevo train station on the very edge of the dacha territory. There isn't an actual station, just a small shop next to the tracks. This became one of my favourite pastimes. With the platform at ground level, people using the trains had to climb up and down using a handrail; when I watched them clambering aboard it reminded me of my own journey on the Trans-Siberian – when the train stopped in remote places, like Pugachevo, where if there wasn't a little shop there was nothing at all. On our journey the train sometimes rested in what seemed like the middle of nowhere. In these obscure and remote locations I felt like I was in the middle of some great adventure where anything could happen and everything was possible. Pugachevo train station evoked these feelings in me without my even possessing a train ticket; although, as it was summer, it looked more like a scene from an old spaghetti western than the white winter voyage I had experienced in 2011. Nastya grew tired of my romantic train obsession and I eventually began walking to the station on my own. Sitting on one of the benches just a few feet from the tracks I became addicted to the rush of adrenalin as cargo trains hurtled past. They had strange Russian symbols on them and company logos that were alien to me. Mostly the wagons carried timber to the west, but occasionally I saw rows of Japanese car transports, nuclear waste containers, tanks, helicopters and various other military hardware en route to Moscow. When they careered down the line and out of view, I would wait for the afternoon passenger trains, because these drew people from miles around. I watched as humans in the distance advanced along the tracks, over the hills and through the forests, while carrying with them sacks of vegetables, pets, or dragging their tired children behind them. It was such a colourful and unusual daily spectacle that even when I wasn't there, if I heard a train in the distance from the dacha I couldn't help but stop and picture it. When I was a boy I had been given a train set by my parents for Christmas, however with our house two sizes too small I never got to set it up properly. It became a dream to see it all fully functioning one day, with my dad forever promising to buy me a large board to set it up on. After my teenage years I lost most of it through moving here and there. The engines were boxed up, the wagons misplaced and the little plastic people never even got to travel to the other side of my bedroom. This inability to see my toy trains move is probably partly to blame for my love of Pugachevo train station. I don't care for train serial numbers or wagon listings, but I am in love with the buzz of life the station attracts and the continual sense of movement.

Evenings at the dacha were often filled with watching episodes of *Friends* and *Desperate Housewives* with Nastya, on a small television linked to a karaoke machine that doubled as a DVD player. As I become more of a dachaman, or *dachnik*, Nastya increasingly liked to watch awful ~~American~~ US TV serials as a way of escape; she may have been born Siberian but for some reason Nastya never fell in love with the old ways of living, preferring instead the metropolitan life of Krasnoyarsk city. Nastya has never gotten to grips with life without a hot shower or soft expensive mattresses, and as punishment for my insistence on us living at the dacha made me watch TV programmes full of people living the ~~American~~ US dream. Often I escaped from this nightmare by writing poetry in a dark corner or reading one of the several translated volumes of Yevtushenko I had brought with me from the UK.

I also spent many evenings outside Dima's dacha, sitting at the table and eating *shashliks*. Marina and Dima usually brought back some chicken or pork with them on their way home from work but it's not unusual in Russia to eat several other types of meat. The rule of thumb seemed to be that if it has more than two legs there is room for it on the barbeque; although we never barbequed horsemeat we did eat it from tins. I thought it strange that a man such as myself, who has spent a considerable chunk of his life in Pentyrch stables tending to the needs of horses, should find himself eating horsemeat in Siberia.

Over the summer, Marina's mother Luda had decided to stay with them. By day she looked out for Semka while Dima and Marina were working, and in the evening they helped prepare food. I didn't fully understand why Luda was staying at Dima's dacha, nor where she had come from but I was thankful because she was quite light-hearted and fun to be around. However, even though Luda was one of the easiest people to be around, as Marina's mother it was clear to see where Marina got her hardness from. Luda gave the impression she was a woman never to be crossed; she had a physical frame a Siberian lynx would be proud of, and I'm sure she had all the same killing abilities to boot.

With Dima's dacha being smaller than Boris's I began to wonder where everyone slept. Semka usually had friends over and they slept on the first floor with him so they could play games, as children do; I therefore assumed that Luda must have slept on the ground floor with Dima and Marina. Their dacha was a very simple design with one main room at the bottom using the stove as a kind of room divider, meaning Luda must have slept only a few feet from her daughter and son-in-law in a toe-to-toe sort of way. This situation was exacerbated when Marina's brother came to stay. Although Vova had a wife and a home to go to, he very often stopped by over the summer to share *shashliks* and beer. Parties got boozy when he was around and lasted well into the early hours as he and Marina bounced off each other like children. It was thanks to Vova that I got to experience the *banya* for the first time. After a night of copious drinking Vova set a fire in the stove of the *banya*, and when it was time, after the stones above the stove had become stupidly hot, he and I went and sat in our pants to sweat our arses off. *Banya* etiquette is another part of Russian life I had to learn. Typically, a fire is set in the stove; this heat then transfers to a number of round boulders in a higher compartment with a bucket of water on top. Inside the bucket are bunches of tied oak, birch or eucalyptus branches that are used to cleanse the skin; it's said that by hitting yourself with these branches circulation is improved. A hat must also be worn to protect from the intense heat, which often reaches 70 °C or more. These hats are usually made from felt and are styled to look like Viking or warrior helmets. With Vova's funny spiked hat, large belly and facial hair he looked a lot like Gerard Depardieu as *Obelix*. Sat in the *banya* in our pants, Vova took it upon himself to show me what the branches were for. He whipped my back several times; with my back already red and sweaty from the searing heat it stung like hell. He wasn't deliberately trying to hurt me, it's normal in Russian *banyas* for people to whip each other's backs and/or any other unreachable parts. To increase the heat Vova used a ladle to throw water on the stones. This caused a build-up of steam that made it absolutely fucking boiling as well as near impossible to breathe. At the point of passing out, Vova motioned for me to follow him to Semka's paddling pool, where the contrast in temperature was heavenly. We lay for a few minutes in the icy cool water before enjoying a sip of beer with everyone on Dima's porch, then repeating the process until we could stand it no longer. Thus my initiation into Russian life was complete, and I became a fully-fledged dachaman. When we finally sat down, tired, whipped and wet, I actually felt really good. My mind was as clear as if I had been for a long run, or eaten a large healthy salad. I could feel all the pistons of my brain firing up and my vision was sharper. This was good because after the *banya* I was expected to last well into the early hours of the morning. Marina, who had enjoyed the spectacle of me running back and forth to Semka's pool asked 'Michael, Cognac, vodka, or tea?' I said I wanted some of all of them, which caused Marina to say 'Ah, you are Russian now.' Because of my initiation, Vova, who had been a little unsure of me before, treated me like an old friend and sometimes slapped my back as old friends do when telling a funny anecdote. This would have been fine if he hadn't been whipping it earlier. Still, I didn't mind. We had washed together, and he had beaten me with sticks, which made us friends.

The Invited

We had been married for over a year and yet my family in Wales had not met Nastya or any other member of my Russian family. Getting Nastya to the UK, even on a tourist visa, was impossible and so the options were limited to meeting in central Europe or my parents coming to Russia. The European option would have been needlessly expensive with hotel and travel costs and there was little chance my disabled mother would even make it to a train station, let alone a foreign country. This left us with only one option: inviting my Dad to visit Russia. We sent him a simple text and he accepted immediately; he would come for Christmas. The only problem we faced was where to stick him; our apartment was small and only had one bed, but I didn't like the idea of him staying with Nastya's parents as they couldn't speak English and he didn't speak Russian; it would have been too awkward for all involved. To solve this Boris agreed to find us a sofa bed small enough to fit into our little kitchen, but big enough to be comfortable, and in return we would give him the stools we currently used to sit at our breakfast table. This exchange of furniture occurs regularly among my Siberian family and friends. For instance, back in December a family friend needed a new bed and my mother-in-law had one just the right size, so she gave her that one; Nataliya Petrovna was then short of a bed, so we gave her ours, then someone had another bed that was perfect for us, and it went around, in a big circle, everyone jostling furniture. Then in summer, I was using an old kitchen table as a desk in our new apartment but Boris came and took it as he needed our spare kitchen table; Boris knew Dima had too many desks in his house and not enough beds, so Boris got me a new desk and sorted Dima with a new bed. I had Dima's desk, Dima had Boris's spare bed and Boris had our kitchen table. The concepts of ownership and property are not taken as seriously in Siberia as they are in the West; communist values are still very much alive. Capitalism has obviously made a dent in Russian culture but it's not fully recognised among some of the older folk. In Siberia we share almost everything. We have some of our own personal things but if someone needs something basic, we pull together and find a way so that no one has to suffer or be without. This doesn't mean there is always peace among my family. They are a passionate people, and with passion comes violence of speech, to the point that it sometimes sounds as if they are at war with one another.

By August, I was quite well adjusted to Siberian life. I felt at home. It was the third month that I didn't need to rush anywhere; still, there were things that I missed. Firstly, my friends and family who seemed to have forgotten me. A friend of mine who had lived in Nicaragua for five years before moving back to Wales and eventually settling in Mumbles, told me that when he lived abroad it felt as if he was in exile, even though he had put himself there. He had felt largely ignored by friends and family, to the point that he wondered if anyone remembered him at all. That is exactly how I felt. I emailed people back in Wales, often with lengthy details of what my life was like, but I usually received replies of 'Yes we're fine here', and not much else. It was as if I had never lived there. I knew it would be difficult living far away and that consequently I would lose touch with some people, but even my best mates and closest family couldn't seem to find time to write back to me, or even Skype for a few minutes.

I should have realised the feeling of exile would envelope me; back in 2006 I had a few friends who left to live in faraway places like Mexico and the US, and to be honest, once they were gone I hadn't thought about them much or contacted them at all. Now it had gone full circle. As well as people, I also missed a great deal of British products. I dearly missed Kellogg's Cornflakes, Rice Krispies and Weetabix. They have similar products in Russia but they are just not the same. I also missed the little, less obvious things like Trebor Extra Strong Mints, Smarties, English mustard, PG Tips, Wine Gums, Oxo gravy granules, and Cornish Pasties; products that are easily taken for granted. The only reminder of home I had was a stuffed cuddly sheep I had brought as a gift for Nastya in March 2011.

When I became visibly sad and homesick Nastya sometimes took me out to eat somewhere nice. Although the majority of contemporary cafés in Siberia didn't agree with me, there were a few that did; especially ones that sold pizza. Yes, who would have thought that Siberians actually knew a lot about pizza? With the inevitable invasion of ~~American~~ US fast food chains following the collapse of the USSR, some Russian businesspersons come up with the idea of starting their own fast food chains; and while the majority of these sell poor excuses for food, there are some that do manage to successfully pull off the fast food experience. It's something I wish I had known during my first couple of visits. There are a few other food products made in Russia that were a total surprise. Firstly, they make great ice cream. There was a time in my life I would have said nothing could beat Thayers of Cardiff but – since they appear to have changed their formula – their ice cream is easily eclipsed by their Russian counterpart. Another surprisingly well-made product in Russia is chocolate. Russians are masters at it, and I say this as a self-confessed chocaholic. In any one of the supermarkets and even some of the smaller shops there are shelves upon shelves full to the brim of different types of chocolate bars and candies. There are so many in fact that I have never managed to buy the same one twice; I want to try them all.

When we weren't at the dacha, Nastya and I sometimes drank a beer in the park near our apartment. This is a common thing to do and the militia don't seem to mind. When it got a bit chilly towards the evening, there was one other place we could go if we felt it was too early to go home. Some of the smaller grocery stores in Krasnoyarsk are slightly unusual in that they don't have cages in them. They are rare but you can find them if you look. In order to survive previous economic meltdowns some of these shops adapted themselves to become bars. I only saw one all summer. It was long rather than wide with a counter running its entire length. Behind this counter were the usual shelves of goods and a shop assistant, but right at the very end were a few stools with shabby, drunken men leaning on the counter. In this place, fellas would come to drown their sorrows over beer that is considerably cheaper than that sold in pubs, because it's still sold at shop prices. The assistant simply removes the bottle top and offers you a stool. We never joined them; but we did buy a beer there to walk home with.

When we were feeling adventurous, we caught a bus to the city centre to visit one of Krasnoyarsk's islands. There are several islands in the Yenisei, the largest of which are Tatysheva and Otdyha Isles. While Otdyha is big enough to house the city stadium as well as a host of other buildings, it is Tatysheva that is often the most visited. Being over twice the size of Otdyha, Tatysheva has become Krasnoyarsk's adventure and exercise island. It has several paths running round its perimeter and through its centre, making it the perfect place to cycle, rollerblade or run. I would say it is probably the only place as Russian roads are chaos. Tatysheva joins the mainland on the north side of the river via a long footbridge which connects directly with Prospekt Mira, Krasnoyarsk's main street. On the mainland side of the bridge there are usually mountain bike and rollerblade rental services in summer, plus a few *shashliks* stalls in case you get hungry. On the island itself there are also outdoor weights and permanent outdoor gym equipment for those who prefer the outdoors to the gym. These facilities are free to use, but they tend to attract well-sculpted men who want to show off their bodies to hot young female things as they rollerblade by.

The island is so big that Nastya and I have only seen the western side of it. To get to the east we would need either to approach it from the eastern bridge or rent a bike. If I had to hazard a guess, I would say the entire city centre would just about fit on Tatysheva with perhaps room enough for Wales and the Titanic.

When crossing the bridge to the island in summer, Nastya and I would often be separated by joggers and cyclists, or small children playing. In accordance with Russian superstition when we met again, after being split up for only a second, we had to greet each other repeatedly. This tended to slow down progress, which is perhaps another reason why we have only seen the western side of the island. As well as this, Nastya developed a habit of hugging me every two minutes. This became known as 'Hugs Time'. Whenever Nastya said this phrase I knew it was time to stop and be squeezed. At first, Hugs Time was quite an annoying concept, as I'm not the most touchy-feely kind of guy and I'm a big fan of walking and exploring, but I got used to it. I think my marriage depended on my getting used to it. Hugs Time is a product of Siberians' heightened sense of romanticism, that I'm sure is already quite well known. I remember watching an episode of *Sex and the City* with my mum one time where the Carrie character dated a Russian bloke who brought too many flowers and liked to hug a lot; she eventually dumped him because of it. The only other Siberian gesture that seemed a bit odd to me was handshaking. In the UK, I have always been accustomed to handshaking at the beginning and end of first meeting someone and occasionally when you see your friends after a prolonged period of separation. In Siberia, men shake hands every time they meet, even if they saw each other only yesterday; and even if they see each other every single day of the year. I've never known anywhere where people are so fond of shaking hands. Although I have not visited every country on Earth, I suspect Siberia is the handshaking capital of the world, which goes to show there is a perfect place for everyone. Growing up in Cardiff everyone knew 'shaky-hands-man', a fella who simply liked to shake hands all day with anyone and everyone on the street, until he died a few years ago. Had he lived in Russia he wouldn't have seemed so odd and out of place. How terrible for him that he was simply born in the wrong country.

Aeroflot Flight SU2578. August 25th 2012. Moscow — London

It was my last flight out of Russia, well I was ninety per cent sure that it would be anyway. One certificate was all that stood in my way. After saying goodbye to Masha in Moscow I thought of how lucky it had been that she had visited Krasnoyarsk over the summer and had to leave at the exact same date as me. I took this to mean that there was some sort of synchronicity taking place in my life. The Gods were with me, even if I didn't believe in them. Sat on the left-hand side of the plane, with a view of the wing, I was anxious. This wasn't due to anything plane related, or anything related to immigration stuff either. I was worried about re-entering the UK because I was expecting to hear even more anti-Russian sentiments from some of my friends since the last time I had seen them due to two highly publicised events that had taken place in August.

On August 15th, an Akula-class Russian attack submarine was reported to have spent several weeks off the Gulf of Mexico in June and July, with the ~~Americans~~ US apparently only becoming aware well after it had left. The Pentagon promptly denied these reports the following day but it was too late, by the afternoon most major Western news agencies had run the story. While this was embarrassing for the US authorities as well as a small victory for Vladimir Putin, it caused unnecessary strain in US-Russian relations and bolstered the negative Russian stereotype at a time when Russia could have done without it. On August 16th, three members of the punk-pop group Pussy Riot were sentenced to two years in prison. This was immediately followed by a glut of anti-Russian propaganda. While I sided with the calls for Pussy Riot's release and fully supported the many online petitions requesting this, what I couldn't condone was the hype being used to make Russia look like some archaic Soviet hellhole. One online petition on Watchdog.com was titled 'Don't let Pussy Riot die in prison' and really offended me for several reasons. Firstly the title – not one of the three convicted members were sentenced to anything longer than two years in prison. Secondly it said 'The prisons in Perm and Mordovia are some of the harshest camps in all Russia, known for severely unhealthy conditions, a complete absence of privacy and a brutal social hierarchy where convicts are subject to abuse and sexual violence by prison guards.' I found myself asking which prison systems do not have unhealthy conditions? And in which prisons do people not get violated regularly? Which prisons do not have a brutal social hierarchy?

Another thing that annoyed me was the completely false propaganda that claimed the jailed members of Pussy Riot were being sent to a Siberian Gulag. Both Perm and Mordovia lie to the west of the Urals, in European Russia, nowhere near Siberia; and Gulags were abolished sometime in the 1950s. When people in the West say the word 'Siberia' they immediately conjure up an image of some vast snow-covered no-man's-land where the sun never shines; but Siberia is actually hot and sunny for half the year and is quite a lovely place to be. Siberia is after all just a place, like Caerphilly or Legoland. Knowing Siberia as well as I do, I find the stereotype of Siberia to be quite offensive. Had Pussy Riot been sent to Cardiff or Swansea Prison people wouldn't have cried out half as much, and yet I believe that the actual loss of freedom and lack of 'privacy' wouldn't have been very different compared to where they were actually sent.

When I spoke to friends online about these glaring untruths, and their obvious use to instill anti-Russian sentiments, I too was met with hostility. It was considered taboo to defend Russia. Even when I made my argument as clearly as I could and presented the evidence above, I was rebuffed with a series of the same untruths and anti-Russian slogans. It was as if I was speaking to robots, who reeled off the same phrases no matter what was said to them. The only other time I can recall having experienced similar hostility and automaton soundbite repetition was when, years earlier, I had tried to talk to a member of the BNP about racism. Some of the people I spoke to about Pussy Riot were academics at the top of their field, and yet they wouldn't even consider anything I had to say or admit that the anti-Russian propaganda was in fact just that. They didn't care if they had their facts right or not, and nor did they care for me trying to fill in the gaps. Russia, and Siberia were now bad places, and it was cool to shout it out. One conversation I can remember with absolute clarity went something like this:

'Perm and Mordovia aren't even in Siberia.'

'So, they're still near it though.'

'They're also near to Central Europe but you don't hate Central Europe do you?'

'What are you on about? They've been sent to Gulags in Siberia not Europe. Don't you read the news?'

'Yes, and both Perm and Mordovia are not in Siberia.'

'What does that matter? What have you got against Pussy Riot?'

By pointing out where information was incorrect I was in danger of being seen as anti-Pussy Riot, which I definitely am not. What struck me the most was that while I was talking to people who were advocating the right to free speech, I didn't feel able to speak freely. Just as I felt it was unsafe to discuss the Pussy Riot trial openly in Russia, I felt equally as intimidated at the thought of discussing it in the UK for fear of being misunderstood.

PART V

Aeroflot Flight SU1481. December 12th 2012. Krasnoyarsk — Moscow

When I woke at 4.30 a.m. I could already hear my dad in the kitchen making tea and coffee. It reminded me of when I had stayed at his house for a while back in 2009. I knew that would be the last time for maybe a year that I would hear my dad boiling the kettle, and the sound of him hitting the teaspoon against the side of the cups. I was happy about the fact we would have our kitchen back again, though it had been real fun with three of us, and an experience we weren't ever likely to live again. Time had flown by too quickly. After taking it in turns to use the bathroom, knock back hot drinks and get dressed, we had to rush outside to where Dima was waiting to drive us to the airport.

On the drive there I berated myself for wasting too much time. I hadn't made the most of my last month with my dad and he had spent a considerable amount of time in the apartment on his own. Now he was leaving. I was also anxious about how he would fare in Yemelyanovo Airport. Without any ability to speak Russian, and no flight calls in English, it was going to be difficult for him to know if he was getting on the right flight to Moscow. Nastya and I had thought about this the night before and discussed trying to attach him to someone on the same flight; or simply making a mental-note of the people in front of us at the check-in desk and getting my dad to memorise them. The problem with these ideas were that we might not find someone kind enough to attach my dad to, and if he had to follow someone Russian, there was the possibility of him losing them. After all Russian people mostly wear dark clothes in December, including big winter coats and hats that all look very alike; so even if we did find someone on the same flight my dad could follow, it would be easy to confuse that person with a hundred other people.

At the check-in desk we found ourselves stood behind some very tall people. All of whom wore blue tracksuits with a little sports logo. Nastya noticed as we waited behind these giants that there was a black man entering the airport, a very rare event indeed. He walked up to the queue, and pushed in just before my dad, which although quite rude was a blessing in disguise. We had hoped there would be someone on my dad's flight who was distinguishable from the crowd. I had even said a few quiet words to the heavens. They answered by sending us the only 7 ft black man we had ever seen in Krasnoyarsk. I took it as being some kind of miracle and told my dad to follow him. We watched as my dad disappeared through check-in then left to find Dima, who had waited in the car because he hadn't been able to find an official parking spot.

Outside, Nastya and I walked along the front of the airport to the big glass doors that were the fire exit of the departure lounge and spotted my dad. He came over to the glass. We communicated in pidgin sign language and writing letters in the ice on the glass. He shrugged his shoulders and turned his head left and right continuously – meaning he couldn't find the bloke he was supposed to be following. I made a frost map of the lounge and pointed him to the café that was around the corner. He hadn't seen it yet. He went there quickly, found the giant man and came back relieved. We made a few funny faces on the frosted glass as a final goodbye. My dad looked really small and vulnerable through that glass. We had taken Boris's big hunting coat and shapka from him at the check-in desk. He was now wearing the grey woollen coat and a beanie hat he had arrived in. We had to leave, not only because of the temperature (-35 °C), but we had to go to the UFMS to register my residency stamp. It was the only day we could do it because we needed Boris, Nataliya Petrovna and Dima to come with us, and Dima was only free on weekends.

Driving away from the airport was a strange experience. I had only ever gone there to leave Siberia. This time I hadn't left the country but had waved someone off instead. In saying goodbye to my dad I had also said goodbye to Wales, my family and my friends. A lump raised in my throat. As we drove past the large red sign welcoming us back into Krasnoyarsk I felt like I was entering new territory.

Dima dropped us at our apartment at around 7.55 a.m. Nastya still had the registration forms to fill out, all four of them. We needed to be at the UFMS at 11 a.m. because they closed at lunchtime on Saturdays. While Nastya was slaving away at the forms in the kitchen, I sat in the bedroom and opened Flightradar24.com on my laptop. This website offers real time satellite coverage for all flights across the globe. I zoomed into focus on Yemelyanovo airport. Nothing came or went for thirty minutes. I asked Nastya if the technology was faulty but she replied that planes can go off radar but only for a few minutes. Never half an hour. If I couldn't see his flight it was because it hadn't taken off yet. My dad was stuck in Krasnoyarsk. I worried about him because he wouldn't be able to understand the announcements, or why his plane wasn't taking off. If two planes left at once in a hurry, he might confuse the two and end up in Vladivostok. Finally, almost an hour late, the SU1481 appeared on the runway. I reasoned to myself that as it was the only plane there my dad would be on it. Now all I had to worry about was him making his connection. Before he left I had drawn him a map of Sheremetyevo airport and had repeatedly told him what it looked like, which corridors were the best and how long it would take. If everything went to plan he would have had one hour and thirty minutes to land, get off the plane, find and follow the path for international transfers, find the lift to the main departure lounge, go to Level 3, walk to the semicircular booth for foreign national transfers, enter customs, face scrutiny, take off his shoes, his belt, his coat; put his keys, wallet and iPod into a little black plastic bucket for screening, and find his plane. But not everything was going to plan: his plane had taken off an hour late, and the weather wasn't brilliant either.

At 10.55 a.m. Nastya and I left to meet her family and go to photocopy the property deeds of our apartment. We waited. At 11.10 a.m. everyone arrived in Dima's car. Instead of driving up the road for one minute, Dima thought it best to drive around a few blocks and approach the UFMS from the back because of ice on the road the way we wanted to go. They stamped my passport. I was given a ten-minute talk on how to obtain a tax number, a work permit and where to go for exit visas, but it was all in Russian and I was too tired to listen to it all. Sat in that office I couldn't really have given a damn about tax numbers, but the hard work was now behind me. I was an actual resident of Siberia. I had the same stamp in my passport that Nastya had in hers. It felt final. I felt secure.

I hadn't realised just how insecure I had felt until that very moment. I had been living in limbo land for a long time. Four times I had left Russia leaving Nastya behind. Four times I had returned to Wales, unsure of where I was going to live. There's a lot to be said for knowing where you're going to be next week or the week after, for being able to leave work on a Friday and go home for the weekend, to be able to go to the cinema on a Saturday night and wake up late on a Sunday, knowing that you have a home to go to, that you belong somewhere. For two years at least I had lived not really belonging anywhere. I had been half in Wales, half in Russia. My mind, soul and actual body had felt torn in two. It was as if I had been living two separate lives and neither of them had been complete. I was exhausted. Walking away from the UFMS I felt free, freer that I had felt in years. To celebrate, Nastya thought we should spend the day at home getting drunk. We bought a bottle of wine and some chicken. It felt strange not being able to share that moment with my father, who was still somewhere 30,000 ft above Siberia, halfway to Moscow.

By the time my dad's flight touched down in Moscow we had finished the wine. I sat in the kitchen, half-drunk, really worried about my dad's situation. He arrived in Moscow at 9.45 a.m. Moscow time (1.45 p.m. Krasno time). His connecting flight to London was due to leave at 10.20 a.m. and had already begun boarding. Because boarding usually closes twenty minutes before take-off, he had fifteen minutes to get off his plane, follow the map I had drawn him, get through customs, find his gate and get on his new plane. It was a tall order. Because he had bought his plane tickets as a set of return package rather than separately, his luggage at Yemelyanovo had been fitted with an automatic transfer ticket, so he wouldn't have to search for it at baggage claim in Moscow. Still, he had a lot to do in a short space of time. Nastya and I stared at the laptop screen, praying he made it. At 10.20 a.m., there was no sign of his plane. At 10.40 a.m., still no sign. At 10.50 a.m. the SU2570 appeared on the runway. It was half an hour late. We were sure my dad was on it; at least we hoped he was. Unlike my trusty pay-as-you-go mobile, my dad had brought his £30 a month, contracted, all singing all dancing touch screen thing with him. Unlike with my phone, my dad needed to talk to his provider before taking a holiday to arrange roaming. He hadn't done this. There was no way he could contact us and vice versa. For all we knew he was still in Krasnoyarsk.

Sat on the sofa where my dad had slept for an entire month, knowing he probably wasn't going to return anytime soon, my sense of freedom slowly turned to sadness and longing. Although my dad is a devout pessimist, moans a lot, hardly ever washed up while he lived with us, and looked like an old sack of potatoes, he was my bag of potatoes, and I was rather fond of having him around. So too was Nastya. We had grown accustomed to the dynamic of having three people in the apartment, and I was used to cooking for more than two. Now the kitchen had a lot more room in it. Once we folded up the bed and turned it back into a sofa, it had even more room. It hit me, sat there, just the two of us that I wasn't going to see my dad again for a long time unless he came back to Russia. I now had three years' residency. I had to find a job, settle in, and make a life for myself. With all the running around – desperation at getting the right certificates, getting to the immigration office on time, getting to Russia, catching the right flights, and making sure I followed the plan – I hadn't taken any time to consider what it would feel like once everything had been achieved. It was a strange feeling. I was now an immigrant, subject to Russian law. All the things I had taken for granted were suddenly so far away. I could no longer pop to Cardiff indoor market and get a breakfast at the Bull Terrier Café, or go to Chapter on a Friday night, get absolutely wasted, stay up till 5 a.m. in Torben's flat singing David Bowie and Peter Gabriel songs and wake up at 2 p.m. the next day not knowing where I was for a few minutes. The beaches of Llantwit Major and Penarth were now more than a short train journey away. My dad and I had gone to Penarth beach so many times. We had skimmed stones and shared any problems we had at the time. I knew that we would likely never share days like that again, and I lamented not having spent more time with him. Nastya felt similar having only known my dad for a month. With the wine finished and no real plans, we spent the rest of the day looking at our photos and trying to remember all the fun we'd had.

Papa in Siberia

After less than three months in the UK, I had found myself sat once again in Heathrow's Terminal 4, only I wasn't alone. After initially agreeing to come for Christmas, my dad had decided it was safer to travel with me in early November and leave in early December, rather than negotiate the various planes and connections on his own. As always when travelling to London from Cardiff I had the hangover from hell after being Torbenated the night before. I was dripping in beer sweat and had a real need for a kebab with all the trimmings. The cafés in Heathrow, like most airports, serve overpriced cardboard similar to old school meals. Thankfully, and typical of my dad, he reached into his breast pocket and produced a plastic bag full of home-made ham sandwiches. I was saved. We left for Moscow on a late morning flight and arrived sometime in the evening. Just like on previous trips there was a wait of several hours in Sheremetyevo before our connecting flight was ready. I used this time to show my dad around the airport. He needed to get familiar with the layout as he would be travelling back on his own. At about 1 a.m. Moscow time we took off from the usual Terminal D in Sheremetyevo. I was weary of this flight due to what had happened on the same flight the previous year. As it turns out I was right to be apprehensive. Soon after take-off our plane started to rattle, and we began to feel weightlessness. This wasn't by any means a normal rattle, and while I know planes usually level out right after taking off, this seemed to go on for too long. After about thirty seconds or so I realised something was wrong and looked at my dad. He had a knowing look. Without saying anything, we were in agreement; the plane was in some sort of trouble. Either gravity had suddenly become stronger or we had lost power. Thankfully the weightlessness subsided, the rattling stopped and the plane started going up again instead of down. Having had a shed load of beer the night before, gotten up at silly o'clock in the morning, caught the National Express to London, and already been on one flight that day, I was totally shattered. I reasoned that if I let myself fall asleep, I would slip into the deepest of sleeps and therefore if the plane went down, I wouldn't feel anything. I woke up just as we were about to land, which thank the lord, went without a hitch. We were met at the airport by Nastya and Dima. After brief introductions, hugs and handshakes we were promptly whisked back to our apartment for tea and eggy-bread. At this point my father seemed too dazed and exhausted to really take anything in. However, neither of us could ignore the fact that we couldn't see through the windows on the balcony. They were iced over. So too were the handles, the runners, even the space between the window that never closes properly and its frame was filled with ice. The entire balcony, instead of being a sanctuary to escape the heat, as it had been in summer, was now a walk-in freezer.

Once Dima had left, we quickly turned the kitchen sofa into its bed shape so that my dad could rest, and everyone including Nastya caught about four hours' sleep.

We were expected at Lilya's at 5 p.m. Dad had no chance of being eased into Russian life slowly. Lilya's hospitality was flawless, and regardless of our lethargic state, neither Nastya nor I wanted to miss her excellent fish. As it was Lilya's birthday, both her daughters had decided to make a surprise visit from Moscow; Masha (with her son Kirill), and Olga, who brought her husband (also named Dima). Lilya's two sisters were also there, as they had been the year earlier. It was quite a sizeable party. I forget how many courses there were but I remember there being more than seven. Every kind of fish cooked in every kind of way, just as it had been the previous December. The difference was that in this party there were also several bottles of vodka, Cognac and champagne. It's not that we got drunk, but after twenty-two hours of travel and only a short period of rest, the copious amount of food alone was enough to make us feel sleepy. We left at about 11 p.m., late enough to have drunk many glasses of good champagne and early enough to avoid the dreaded karaoke.

As this was my dad's first time in Russia we wanted to make a good impression, however, due to the size of our apartment, and the fact that it has only one bedroom (which is also our living room), my dad was relegated to sleeping in the kitchen. He was relatively comfortable, as the sofa bed was large enough and stuck right next to the radiator. If anything, because of the lack of ventilation, he was too hot during the nights. This situation may sound overcrowded, but it was luxury compared to how Dima had been living. Over the autumn period – while I was away in the UK sorting out my new criminal records certificate – Marina's brother Vova, her mother Luda, and Marina's pregnant daughter Natasha, from a previous marriage, all moved into Dima's apartment. I'm not sure what their reasons were. Vova apparently fell out with his wife, Natasha fell pregnant by someone who nobody really knew and consequently she needed some assistance; and as for Luda, there was apparently some discomfort in that she lived with her mother, and wanted to be further away from her. By comparison our apartment felt roomy.

The winter was much colder than the last one. When I arrived with my dad in Krasnoyarsk the temperature was -5 °C, but by the time he left it was -35 °C, though we had experienced a few days of -38 °C. Because of this shocking cold, we had to wear more layers than I had the previous years. The day before we left the UK, I had gone to my dad's house to inspect his luggage. I had made him a list and made sure he had packed everything I suggested: three pairs of thermals, several jumpers, snow boots, undershoe ice grips that fit to the boots, a hat or two, a set of thermal gloves. My dad was prepared in every way except for his coat. I had instructed him to bring his long woollen winter coat that he would normally wear over a suit if he was attending a posh do; it felt really warm and heavy in Wales, in Russia however it was like paper. I didn't realise until at least a week after arriving that my dad was in fact freezing his arse off. Thankfully Boris was kind enough to lend my dad a real fur shapka and a large black cotton hunting coat that could handle temperatures as low as -40 °C.

In our apartment, like in all old Russian city apartments, the heating stays on constantly in winter and cannot be turned off. It's controlled by the central heating system elsewhere in the city and is piped to every building. This makes all apartments a bit stuffy; because my dad was sleeping next to the radiator in the kitchen, and because he couldn't open the windows of the balcony, he slept really awfully throughout his visit. Several times he opened the door to the balcony just a fraction, but this injected the kitchen with too much cold air in a matter of seconds. The ice on the inside of the window frames got thicker every day, eventually becoming more than an inch thick in places. Due to the stuffiness of our apartment, and the lack of sleep, my Dad was more lethargic than I had ever seen him; some days he even slept in till about midday. Taking a shower didn't help either. Our shower room has no ventilation, so when you step out of the shower it's near impossible to get dry with the buildup of steam. Even if you do manage to get dry, the constant heating soon has you wet with perspiration. This may have been why my father took fewer and fewer showers throughout the month. Like in summer, we sweated like pigs.

In our apartment, the only way one can wake up fully and escape the oppressive heat of the apartment is by going outside. However, this isn't simply a case of popping your shoes on. To go anywhere in Krasnoyarsk in winter you have to prepare as if you were going on some major arctic expedition. You must ensure you have several layers on your legs, two pairs of thermal trousers, thermals on the upper body, a jumper, your coat, gloves, a scarf, and you must never ever forget your shapka. With all these clothes on, you sweat horrendously before you even step out the door. This makes the Russian tradition of sitting for a few moments of silence before you take a long trip even more tedious.

Rambo

Stepping through the large door to exit our apartment building is also a bit of an experience in sub-zero temperatures. Firstly the door is iced over, on the inside. Blades of ice run right across giving the impression that Jack Frost or some huge snow beast got its hands caught as the door was closing. It regularly sticks the door to the frame but in winter, after pressing the button to release the magnetic lock I would have to throw myself against it shoulder first. Once the door is open we then move outside onto the small porch with four steps that lead down to ground level. Because the snow is relentless the steps have a kind of outdoor heating system of their own to keep them from turning into a slide. A generator sits below the building that forces steam out of a pipe underneath the steps and out through the gaps in between them. This steam is quite harmless by the time it rises above the steps, but it builds up around the outside of the doorway, so that when we open the main door, all the steam rushes in. There is so much of it that for the first few minutes you can't see, and it's all the worse if you have sunglasses on to protect you from snow glare.

When the steam clears, the initial view outside is snow – in the sky, on the ground and on the rooftops of every building. Every morning in Krasnoyarsk, a team of municipal workers have to go out to clear snow from paths and stairwells. As we are in the suburbs our building isn't serviced in this way therefore the path is only made visible by people's feet. Hence our entrance path is barely visible in winter. There are several dangers when stepping out of our building. First, you have to make sure there isn't ice where you want to walk. Most Siberians make a mental note of the path and plan their movements ten steps ahead. The ice is usually more reflective and is easy to avoid. Secondly, when you leave any building you must look up to check if there are any icicles. These can be anything from a few inches to several feet in length. They can kill and so you must always be aware of them. During the middle of the day when the sun is up they can become weak and occasionally fall. On days when Nastya was working and my dad and I were sat in the kitchen, we would sometimes be distracted by what sounded like gun fire. We discovered that it was caused by icicles falling from the guttering onto the steel windowsills. The icicles are not a permanent danger, they occur at the beginning of winter, because the temperature increases enough to melt snow, but in the middle of winter, once they have fallen under their own weight, they are no longer anything to worry about. After that it doesn't warm up enough for snow to melt, and icicles are not seen again until the warmer weather comes in April. The third danger is that you have to watch out for the hounds of Siberia. These beasts are ordinary dogs; however, with their wild fur coats and wolf-like eyes they often give the impression of being some weird hybrid beast. They come in various colours and sizes but what they all have in common are sharp claws and long teeth. They can work in packs but some stand alone. For the most part they are friendly, but if you have recently eaten meat and still have the smell of it on your hands they can turn on you. When they growl and hiss they can be very intimidating. We have one at the bottom of the footwell of our building. He is half the size of me but with his large brown coat looks more like a bear. Over the course of the month my dad was in Siberia I made a point of making friends with this hound. Dog, as I had so affectionately named him would not only come to me when I called, but would follow me to the local shop and then wait to walk me home again. The fourth and final hazard to look out for, as you step out into Siberia, are the people. For the most part Siberians are harmless and lovely but there are some bad eggs wherever you go. There have been a few drunk people who congregate outside our building, just standing there with a bottle of something. I've never had any problem from them but you never know. There can be as many as five drunks just hanging round the main entrance. Sometimes they come in, maybe to get a few minutes' warmth. It's possible that they live in the building, like us. Still, I never speak English around them and I made sure my dad was aware that he should do the same. There are times in Siberia when native English speakers should keep their mouths shut. There are times when native Russians should keep silent too. While walking down the street during my first couple of visits Nastya sometimes told me to be quiet. She did the same with my dad only he didn't take it as well as me. He demanded an immediate explanation and I had to be the one to tell him to 'Shut the fuck up'.

Nastya, being a home-grown Siberian, has a heightened sense of danger. She can sense when someone is lying, when someone has bad intentions and when someone nearby has possible ill will towards foreigners. She is right on most occasions. To us Brits it can occasionally seem excessive, but such hyper-awareness isn't always a bad thing. In Siberia, in summer but more so in winter, you learn to keep your eyes and ears open at all times. If you are on the street you have to learn to be prepared for danger but without showing it; and though you train your eyes and ears to be on full alert you must also let your primary senses subside, and let your intuition or second sense come to the front of your mind. Russia is a mystical place, and the people believe in all kinds of mysterious crap. The only part of this that is real for me is learning to live by my gut feeling. It now serves me more than my eyes and ears. Sometimes, for apparently no reason, the hairs on my arms rise. They spike up like some kind of human radar system. And I listen to the feeling, that isn't in my mind, but in the whole of me. It's like learning to walk all over again, only the dangers aren't things you see or hear, smell or taste. They are in the shadows, or they are the shadows themselves. This is something I tried desperately to get my dad to understand, but being an old and rather stubborn know-it-all, he wasn't having any of it.

Before bringing my dad to Russia, one of my concerns was how he would mix in, and whether he would be able to obey the certain unwritten rules we have that keep us safe. Back in Wales, my dad likes to convey a hard-man image. He keeps his head shaved (though I think this is perhaps to mask the bald patch on top of his head that happened in his early twenties); he grunts a lot and speaks very loudly. Also, because he's been a builder for at least thirty years, he's pretty well-built for a British person. Back when he was twenty, he studied several martial arts, ran a few marathons, and lifted weights. By UK standards I suppose he is a bit of a hard-man. Compared with the standard of Russian men, however, my dad is as hard as a sack of mouldy old potatoes. During his month in Siberia, when he stood alongside Russian men, he did indeed look a lot like a sack of potatoes with a Mr Potato Head face on top. Not that my dad is terribly unfit now, compared to who he was in his twenties, but you have to remember that Russians usually take excellent care of their bodies, and the harder living conditions and dacha lifestyle make them very tough people. Not only are the regular, law-abiding citizens built like Dolph Lundgren, but there are also a number of law-flouting citizens: drunks, thieves, mafia, and mafia subordinates. I suppose Krasnoyarsk, like everywhere in Russia and the rest of the world, has its own mafia. While walking with my dad, we often passed a number of cars without number plates. Whereas in the UK, these would be instantly spotted and stopped by police, in Russia the police seem to ignore them. Although I couldn't say for sure if those cars and the people in them were part of any organised gangs, owing to the fact their vehicles were in open violation of the law I thought it best never to look at the people inside or around them, and instructed my dad to do the same.

There is a rather shady nightclub near our apartment. By day it looks like a regular café, although, unlike most other cafés and clubs this building stands detached from everything else on the corner of a main road. I have never been inside but have heard horrendous stories about this place. According to Nastya, there are regular fights there in the evening and unassuming people who have visited the club have either been stabbed or seriously wounded. It has all the characteristics of a nightspot that should be shut down, and yet it isn't. Though it sounds a lot like a few establishments in the UK, I can't think of one nightclub in Britain that I would be afraid to walk past during the day. Knowing all this, you can imagine my alarm when my dad told me one evening that the local hard men 'don't seem to like it when you stare back at them.' I casually explained to him in the best way I could that, even though in his mind he is a hard-man, he'd get no extra points for getting himself killed. The British embassy is closer to Cardiff than Krasnoyarsk, and if he was hurt, it's likely nobody around would help. There is no shame in looking away when a Siberian hard-man stares you out. It's not cowardice, simply self-preservation. My dad listened to me and mumbled something that sounded like agreement but I knew deep down he would still stare at local hard-men. I only hoped that he didn't annoy the wrong person before he was due to leave. Had my dad stared at the wrong person, there was no knowing what could have happened.

North Korea Invades

Within a few days of arriving back in Krasnoyarsk I received a letter in the post from Siberian immigration. I had been granted temporary residency for three years. The type of residency I was given meant I could only live in Krasnoyarsk unless I could prove a means of sustaining myself elsewhere. All I had left to do was get my new certificate of no criminal record – which had recently been granted to me by Cardiff Police Station – translated and notarised, together with its Apostille, and get a new 'I don't have Aids' certificate. This meant I had to go back to that clinic again, and be crammed into a room full of scary-looking people. Getting the translation was a piece of cake; an office in the city centre took care of it overnight. Obtaining a new HIV certificate was going to be the headache it had been in summer. Early one morning Nastya and I went to the clinic to register, as we had done a few months earlier. Because we got there at about 11 a.m. and the taking of blood happened at 4 p.m. sharp, we decided to hang around the centre that day. It was -28 ˚C. We ate a lukewarm potato pie and then washed it down with piss-poor tea in every café we could afford to enter.

At 4 p.m., frozen, we went back to the clinic. On this occasion there was a battalion of men in matching camouflage clothes, the kind Boris wears. These men were short but extremely well built. They didn't speak in any language I recognised. It turned out they were all from North Korea. Even though my name was above theirs on the list, they were processed first as one large group. It seemed no one wanted to argue with them. The following day we went back for my results and certificate and, because we had left my dad alone in our apartment for ages the day before, we thought it best to take him with us. At the very least he would get some fresh air. He needed stamps for his postcards and wanted to visit a post office anyway. We left late. After visiting the post office, getting no less than four stamps for each postcard, licking them as fast as we could, sticking them on and throwing them in the first postbox we found, we arrived at the HIV clinic.

Nastya had worked a nightshift and rushed to the clinic in the morning to put my name down first. Because of this we didn't have to wait long. When my name was called, Nastya and I squeezed ourselves through the would-be-assassins, past the guard and into the certificate office. My dad would have to stay and wait for us. As I left that room I looked back at him and hoped he kept his hard-man stare to himself. Once we had the certificate and I had been given a lecture I didn't understand but can only assume was about how important it is still to use condoms and be a good boy, we grabbed my dad, bought some cakes at my favourite patisserie near the Krasnoyarsk Hotel on Central Square then caught a bus home. All we needed now was an appointment at the immigration office.

Hypothermia

Unlike the previous winter, this year's cold was earlier and slightly more extreme. Within two weeks of our arrival it had quietly gone from -5 °C to -25 °C, with occasional days of -31 °C. There was no room for error when we went out. With all my attention focused on making sure my dad was covered up properly, I made the schoolboy error of neglecting myself on more than one occasion. Three times during the month I left the apartment without my shapka. Although this was easily fixed, as soon as I stepped outside I was instantly reminded that my head was uncovered, and even if I didn't go back for my shapka, my jacket has a hood that would have been more than adequate for a few hours. One day however, while we were planning a trip to the local outdoor market, just five minutes from our apartment, I had neglected to put sufficient cover on my legs. I wore one pair of thermals and one pair of thick trousers. I had also failed to notice that I had a crack in the rubber of my snowboots. Needless to say I got ill. We got to the market without incident and spent a good thirty minutes looking round. Nastya and my dad were talking about taking a ten-minute walk up the road to buy some of the same tea towels we had at home (for some reason my dad took a fancy to Siberian tea towels). During this time, it seemed that I had become increasingly irritable and nauseous. I told them both that I felt a bit cold and that my toes were cold, but they didn't realise just how freezing I was. After five more minutes at the market I felt something strange at the core of me. It felt like I had begun to disintegrate from the inside out. I mentioned this to Nastya, who, after telling me how stupid I was decided on a course of action. We would go to see Boris, as he would know better than anyone how to make me feel better and would also be able to lend me some snowboots without holes in. When we got to Nastya's parents' apartment, I had to take off my shoes and socks and sit with my feet in a bowl of water. The temperature of this water was then increased gradually. My legs were extremely cold. It took nearly an hour for the warmth to creep up into my body. While sat in this funny position, I was also made to drink hot water. Lots of hot water, and made to eat hot fish pie. As it turned out, it wasn't such a bad experience. The fish pie was excellent and being pampered was something I could get used to. When we left Boris to go home again, with me wearing a pair of Boris's old boots, I made a promise to myself never to be so stupid again. I had worn several layers, but had made the mistake of underestimating the cold and not speaking out soon enough when I knew something was wrong.

Siberians don't spend their entire time outside when they are wearing all these clothes. They do all the same things that people do everywhere else, like visiting shopping centres, friends' apartments, cinemas and cafés. And, just like our apartment, all of these places have the heating on permanently. As you can imagine, in a hot building with four or five layers, Siberians sweat heavily unless they are in a place where they can strip off a few items. There are several consequences of sweating so much. The worst of these is something I'm sad to say I have experienced.

With thermals, pants, trousers and long coats on, the part of the body that heats up the most is the groin. I think this problem may be worse for men although I can't say for certain. You must remember that the man rocket area was specifically designed to hang loose outside the body, because man rockets and their accompanying parts are supposed to be a few degrees cooler than the rest of the body. When they are forced to live in an environment that is too warm for them, they can become slightly unfriendly to the nasal senses. There must be some kind of medical term for this but the only name I know is one given by the Americans: jock itch. It may sound funny but during the increasingly harsh winter, I noticed that when I got home and stripped down, there was an odour of the unwanted variety. On closer inspection in the bathroom mirror I was alarmed to see that the skin around my man parts looked slightly distressed. After a quick Google search I discovered that this particular problem was common among athletes and men who work in warm places, like steel factories and bakeries. People have long debated the best way forward in curing it, E45 cream and hydrocortisone are both popular, but what I found to be the most effective way in making sure my man parts are happy is by putting on some big shorts in the evening that allow everything to hang loose. I later learned that Siberian men avoid this situation by wearing baggy thermal trousers. I had been wearing skintight thermals. Not long after I went to the shop and invested in a pair of the lovely baggy thermals – one of the best investments I've ever made.

The Italian Way

I was impressed by how unfazed my dad had been by Siberian life. He hadn't felt any of the fear I had known on my first visit. At times, he seemed to actually prefer the Russian way of life to his own. Though while Nastya was on a nightshift and we had time to talk, he expressed annoyance at being told to not speak English. 'What's the worst that could happen?' and 'Why isn't Russia more like Spain or Italy?' were questions I heard all too often. In fact Nastya and I both became quietly irritated as my father increasingly asked why things weren't more Spanish or Italian. I think he had some kind of dual culture shock due to the fact he had been on holiday in Spain just two weeks before arriving in Russia. As for the Italian fixation, that had more to do with the fact his best mate from Cardiff, in fact the one he had gone to Spain with, was an Italian fella. My dad has never been to Italy. Regardless of this fact, he relentlessly kept comparing everything he ate with Italian food. As Siberia was considered an alien place to his friends back in Cardiff, he had been asked to keep a diary, which he did every day. By the end of his stay he was nearing five thousand words. This was later reduced down into article shape and subsequently published by *The Siberian Times*. In this article, my dad listed his favourite things, such as the traffic system (all traffic lights run on a digital timer, so every driver and pedestrian knows how long they have to wait), the lack of Americanisation and culture of litigation currently ravaging the UK, and he dedicated a whole paragraph to Russian kitchen designs. There was no mention of Italy or Spain, and no mention of our apartment door either, which I think was an oversight because my dad complimented our front door nearly every time we left or entered the apartment.

In the third week of my father's stay we were woken up at about 5 a.m. by the sound of grinding and cutting equipment in the floor above us. It went on for about an hour with much cursing, screaming, and the general sounds of someone who is extremely pissed off. How this person had locked themselves out is unfathomable, seeing as you have to have a key in your hand to lock the door anyway. I can only assume they lost their key while out on the tiles and needed to remove their apartment door and frame to get to the spare. We had to explain to Nastya that it wouldn't happen in the UK as most front doors have glass in them, are made of plastic or wood or have pick-able locks. I don't think she believed us. It's impossible for someone who has spent almost all of her life in such a security conscious country to imagine a world with wooden or plastic front doors. Although dachas usually have wooden doors, it's uncommon for people to leave any valuables in them. During the winter people half expect them to be broken into, but don't worry about it as there's little left to steal; televisions, karaoke machines and microwave ovens are ferried back and forth every year without fail.

After my dad's first week in Krasnoyarsk, we had covered the basics and more. We had visited my favourite museum, attended a party at Lilya's, eaten in cafés every other day, visited the city centre several times and made sure we had wine and beer in the apartment every evening. The only problem was that we didn't have an everlasting pile of cash. I had brought a few hundred quid from Wales but there wasn't much left after the first week. For the remaining three weeks we had less to live on that we had spent in the first week. Although my dad had brought his own money and plenty of it, we didn't want to be poor hosts. Nastya and I discussed it one evening in bed and decided we would have to introduce my dad to the Siberian way of living. I wasn't sure how my dad was going to make this transition without feeling some sort of major culture shock so I did my best to make meals my dad wouldn't find too different. We had a stock of deer meat in the freezer, which I used to make meatballs to accompany spaghetti, and I crushed tomatoes and garlic to make pasta sauces. Occasionally we went to eat at Nastya's parents' place. We got by but after the first week of tourist attractions, mountains and daily outings I was afraid my dad would get bored. We didn't have a television and there was literally no place my dad could hang out comfortably other than the kitchen. I went through my books and selected a few of the English-language novels I had brought from the UK. My dad chose Aleksandr Solzhenitsyn's *The First Circle*. He finished it within two weeks. As I was on the lookout for a job, Benya arranged a meeting with the CEO of the company she worked for. Benya's boss had a reasonably decent grasp of English and knew a few language teachers who might be able to set me up with something. We arranged a meeting in a café close to Nastya's office on a freezing cold morning. My dad and the CEO seemed to make some sort of romantic bond straight away. They flirted like hell. I was a bit embarrassed at first, but then I realised it was a mutual attraction and let them get on with it. They started going on day trips together although I had to escort my dad to the rendezvous point. Nastya and I felt a bit guilty about not being able to show my dad around ourselves, but those day trips took the pressure off us and we were finally able to spend some time at home alone.

The downside to this was that while my dad was out with his new lady friend, she began falling for him. This wasn't good because my dad hasn't had a serious relationship since my parents divorced in 1997, and I know him well enough to say he will never get married or settle down ever again. His lady friend didn't know this and I suspected, if she was anything like Nastya, that the day trips with my dad would have some huge romantic significance. Friendships in Siberia tend to be male with male, or female with female; rarely do men have female friends. They have female colleagues and distant cousins who they can hang out with but the concept of a male/female friendship for friendship's sake isn't widely understood in Krasnoyarsk, or at least as far as I can see. As a result of these two very different cultural attitudes, my dad's Siberian lady friend became quite offended when he didn't reciprocate her advances. I knew it would happen and tried warning my dad about it, but being his usual stubborn self he said 'It's just a casual meet up like. If they don't know casual here yet

212

they're gonna have to learn it sometime, and it might as well be from me.'

Stamps, Stamps, Stamps and More Stamps

The only problem we had experienced with regard to my immigration was with the Certificate of No Criminal Record, in that I had obtained the wrong one earlier in the year. But now I had a new certificate that wasn't only issued in the UK from the British Police authority but was recommended to me by the British High Commission. It couldn't fail. One morning when Nastya had finished a nightshift, she made a special trip at 8 a.m., straight after work, to pick up the certificate and its translation from the office we'd left it at in the city centre. I didn't know of this of course, until I received a phone call from Nastya at the immigration office tearfully telling me I had brought the wrong certificate again. At the bottom of my new certificate it stated that it cannot say whether I am a person of good character but that I definitely did not have a criminal record. Apparently this wasn't good enough. They needed something that said I was of good character. I argued that it was bullshit and if the immigration service looked at the British Foreign Office website they would see that the UK doesn't give certificates of good character or good behaviour because they mean absolutely nothing. I stressed that according to Russian law, an immigrant must provide proof they do not have any criminal convictions in their native country, and I had indeed provided solid proof of that. Certificates stating someone is not an arsehole are not a legal requirement. Thankfully, they did have a look on the website and saw I was right.

A few days before my dad was due to leave, Boris collected Nastya and me to take us to the immigration office. We didn't need an appointment because I had a letter that said I had been granted residency. We took every certificate, copies of every certificate, our passports, notarised copies of my brain scan, written consent of everyone currently living in Russia, written consent of everyone living outside of Russia, a chest X-ray certificate, a leprosy certificate, a bubonic plague certificate and a pear tree. We arrived early which was just as well as all of the would-be assassins we had seen at the HIV clinic were already there. There were pear trees everywhere. When our turn came, we went into the little interview booth and handed over the pile of documents that was now about as tall as I was. They took my passport and inspected it closely. Thankfully, the picture of me inside looked enough like me to pass scrutiny. Then they began inspecting the pile of documents. Weeks went by. I grew a lengthy beard that made me look like one of the guys from ZZ Top, though thankfully I'd had the foresight to take an electric razor with me. Crammed into the little booth with our pear tree it was a bit of a tight squeeze. Branches were sticking out of the door, which meant it couldn't be locked. People kept opening the door and trying to get in because they were dying of old age too. When my documents had been inspected, a very senior looking official came out to inspect my pear tree. It was fine, slightly bent, but fine. However, I had forgotten the bloody partridge. Nastya ran outside and told Boris who had one spare in the glove compartment of his car. We were saved. They took the partridge, stamped it and put it in my file. After this process had been repeated with everyone in the waiting room, a tiny slip of a woman in six-inch heels came out from behind the booths and unlocked a door in the little waiting room. Behind that door was a 4 ft tall fingerprinting machine. Everyone had to have their fingerprints, palm prints and thumb prints recorded eighteen thousand times. It took twelve years to process everyone. When it came to my turn, the tiny woman, who could have only been two inches wide at the waist, gave me back my passport. Nastya opened it – on the middle page it had the stamp we had been waiting so long for. It had taken five trips to Russia, nineteen flights, and hundreds of hours of anguish to obtain. We went back to the car where Boris had waited the whole time. On the drive home I couldn't help grinning because I was now a legal resident of Russia. Only I wasn't. Nastya told me that I needed a stamp to validate the stamp, and in order to obtain the second stamp I would need to go to local immigration office within the next seven days. Plus I would need to take Nastya and all of her family with me, as well as all of her dead ancestors going back fifty years. I held my head in my hands and sighed.

By this time the temperature was beginning to level off at -35 °C. During the night it could get as low as -39 °C. It hadn't yet bottomed out at -40 °C but it would soon. It was now hard to distinguish roads from pavements. All the snow from the roads that had been swept towards the verges now formed large solid snow banks. The only time we knew we were crossing a highway is because it had two banks either side, otherwise they were white with occasional tyre tracks that snow would quickly cover over. Outdoor staircases now looked like ski slopes. Only well-traversed stairs would be swept every day. Emergency stairways coming from office blocks were now ice slides. On days when Nastya was working, my dad and I would stay home and talk. When Nastya's shift finished my dad and I would leave the apartment at 7.20 p.m. exactly. This gave us forty minutes to reach Nastya's office. In the extreme cold of -35 °C, when we exited the building we had to take a few seconds for our bodies to adjust. In such temperatures the body finds it hard to breathe, it feels as though the chest is under pressure. Icicles form on the nose hairs and frosty eyelashes begin to seal the eyes closed. Hands must be gloved up and at least three pairs of socks worn. The shapka should have the side whiskers lowered to cover the ears, or they will freeze and fall off.

My father and I are both reasonably fit people. Back when I was twenty-five (not all that long ago), we would walk up Pen y

Fan every Sunday afternoon. We were so fit at one point we could walk up to the top and get back down to the car within an hour and thirty minutes. In Krasnoyarsk, in winter, walking to an office forty minutes away, it felt as though we were both eighty. Within five minutes of walking our pace decreased to a slow dragging, and by the time we reached the office we were both knackered. A walk like that is nothing to my father-in-law. Those regular treks to the office really gave my father and me some perspective about what shape our bodies were in. I think my dad realised he wasn't the *Rambo* type he thought he was. This made me sad. I didn't like hearing my dad admit how the cold affected him. I think this is because I found comfort in him being a kind of hard-man. I had only experienced this once before. Back in 2008 when I was planning a cycle ride from Brecon to Cardiff in winter, after it had snowed, my dad turned down the opportunity of riding with me. He said that he didn't think he could make it. Faced with Boris's prowess and exceptional level of fitness I think my dad began to feel old in Siberia, and I began to see him that way too. On nights when Nastya was doing an 8 till 8 nightshift, I would lie in bed and listen to the radiator. We have two radiators in our bedroom and one of them makes a low humming sound, like the sound of machinery in the distance. I associate this sound with the Soviet Union – the general hum of factories that never stop working. Some nights I would lay awake and contemplate what would happen if the humming stopped and the heating ceased. In those moments I worried about my dad more than ever. There was no way the heating would shut down however there was no longer *any* way I could ignore the cold hard truth that the *Rambo* of Cardiff was getting old.

The Abominable Snowman

Two nights before my dad was due to leave, Nastya and I had arranged a party of sorts. We hadn't any money for alcohol but thought it would be nice to attempt to cook a traditional Sunday roast and have a dinner party for the three of us. On hearing about this, Nataliya Petrovna, Boris and Dima somehow invited themselves over. Although, true to form we only got one of Nastya's parents; Boris came without Nataliya Petrovna because they had been bickering over his hunting equipment lying around their apartment. The chicken dinner I prepared worked out quite well, regardless of the fact I only had three hobs to work with. The gravy was a bit of an experiment. I made a base from onions and procured some beef stock from a shop near Nastya's work. It came together better than I thought it would. Boris seemed to love it. For a man who tends to be choosy in what he eats he ate quite a lot. He brought a bottle of red wine with him. It was the first time I ever saw Boris drink. Dima arrived later, but the wine had gone by then.

After everything had been consumed, and the plates close to licked clean, Boris and Dima engaged in some sort of debate, which lasted for two hours. Dima was trying to convince his father that there was an afterlife as well as some sort of mystic theory he was working on. According to Dima, astral projection was something that could be attained through practice. Boris was having none of it, as I expected. Boris very calmly gave a counter argument that the world we see is the world we have, that rivers flow towards the sea, gravity pulls things downwards, time spent thinking about astral worlds, and life after death was time wasted. I was surprised however, when Boris told everyone that he believed in Big Foot. This was very unusual behaviour for a man who refutes any and everything remotely sensational or spiritual. He gestured with his hands that he had seen a footprint the size of a man's upper body. As a non-believer, I must have pulled a face that conveyed my feelings. I have one of those faces that always says what I'm thinking even if I keep my mouth shut. Seeing this, Boris thought for a moment, then rationalised aloud that the footprint he saw could have been a bear's. But I knew he was saying this to save face in front of me and my dad. What he had initially said could not be unsaid. Even Boris, the most straight thinking, down-to-earth, rational man I had ever met couldn't help but be influenced by all the mystical talk that goes on in Siberia. Little did I know that this was only the tip of the ice yeti. There was more to come.

The following night we had another dinner party. This time Nastya cooked. My dad had given us a Boney M wall clock and 5000 roubles (£100) as a Christmas present so I could buy some decent snow boots. We spent 500 roubles on wine for that final evening. Boris and Dima invited themselves over again, this time bringing Nataliya Petrovna with them. As it was a special occasion Nastya's parents put their petty arguments aside and made an effort to be civil. The night was very much similar to the one prior. Nataliya Petrovna brought some stewed cabbage, and boiled horsemeat with potato. It was a lot of food and a lot of wine. It didn't take long for our conversations to wind down the path of mysticism once more. This time we came upon the topic of apocalypse. This subject is quite a common one in Russia. There are television programmes about the impending end of the world at least once a week, and the idea is that in the event of a global disaster, Siberia would be the only place on Earth left unscathed. It sounds like madness, but millions of people actually believe it, including Nastya. The one person I hadn't expected to believe a word of it was Boris. There had been a lot of hype in the media, more than usual in fact, because of the Mayan calendar theory. The world was due to end on the 21st of December. Exactly two weeks away. Nataliya Petrovna and Boris told us that they were planning to spend the end of the world in the dacha, and stay there for at least three or four nights. To try to convince us that they hadn't gone totally bonkers they explained that with so many people believing in the end of the world, there would likely be some panic in the city and so it was best to stay well away. Boris had bought extra supplies of nearly everything needed to survive an apocalypse: vegetables, salt, medicines and bullets. He had actually gone all over the city looking for extra supplies of bullets because people had begun to panic-buy them, as well as guns of every kind. I kind of saw their rationale for leaving the city. I didn't like the sound of all the bullets and guns being sold out. Who knows who would be carrying what? As a final measure Boris was planning a hunting trip one week before apocalypse day; they needed a whole deer just in case the apocalypse lasted more than one week. With all this talk of the end of the world, I was expecting Nastya or Dima to invite themselves along to the dacha, but they didn't. They both had to work that day, and Nastya even had a nightshift on the 21st. Regardless of the impending end of everything, they would make sure the good people of Siberia were able to get online right up to and including the moment the four horsemen made their appearance.

If we survived the end of the world, Dima told us he would still be spending January on his own at his dacha, as he had done every year since he could remember. The -40 °C to -45 °C temperatures predicted weren't going to put him off. I felt like asking him if this was also a way of escaping the family, especially seeing as Marina had moved most of her family in with them, but I didn't. He would have denied it anyway and it would have probably been an insensitive thing to do. I wondered whether being at the dacha in sub-zero temperatures made him feel closer to his father in some way. With Boris forever going back and forth to the taiga, he comes across as being a man's man. Dima however, with his white-collar job and shiny office shoes, has become hunched from hours sitting at desks and pushing pens. I got the impression that although they loved each other, they weren't that close. It was possible that Dima's month-long session in the dacha during the coldest period may have been a way of bolstering his father's respect. Whatever his reason, it wasn't my place to question. Apocalypses and freezing evenings spent in dachas aside, it was an enjoyable evening, though all the talk of the end of the world on what was essentially the last evening I would spend with my dad made me feel a greater sense of finality; it really felt like the end of an era.

HIRAETH AND THE APOCALYPSE

Being a resident of Cardiff most of my life I had visited Cardiff Castle more than a thousand times and had a permit which allowed me to get in for free. I even had my first date there. On summer days, I would buy a Brie and bacon baguette from the small café opposite the castle gates on the corner and take it to the castle, together with a coffee from the market. I would stand on top of the castle, eat my lunch, and look at all of South Wales as if it were mine. It was mine. Mine to enjoy whenever I felt like it. The museum, the barrage, the Bay, Bute Park, the peacocks of the castle, the nightclubs, the Nos Da backpackers' bar next to the river, these things were mine. Now they were out of reach. Over the course of two or three years, I had struggled with my sense of national identity. I always felt like a tourist in Cardiff, partly because I had lived in Abertridwr during my teens and Pentyrch during my early twenties. At those crucial times when I should have been discovering my own city, I had gone off to discover other places in Wales. In addition, because I had failed my Welsh A-level, and cannot speak Welsh fluently, I felt like I did not belong, like there was something missing from my life that could only be found outside of Wales. It was on that first day of being a Siberian resident that I realised I was not only a half Russian-half Brit... I was not merely an expat, an immigrant, or an honorary Siberian; I was a Welshman. A Welshman in Krasnoyarsk, and even though I had left my homeland far behind, I could still wake up every morning and thank the Lord that I was Welsh.

According to Russian superstitions if you clean your house within three days of a guest leaving they will have a bad journey home, or they will die, or devils will come, big Russian-speaking devils that want to force-feed you kittens. I didn't want this to happen but it was difficult after my dad had left to leave the kitchen the way it was. The floor hadn't been cleaned in a month, and as the sofa bed was a sofa once again, we found dust-bunnies so big there was a danger of them turning into dust-bears or tigers. I had to clean, just a little bit. Three days after my dad had left, we Skyped each other. He had panicked in Yemelyanovo Airport just as I had thought. He had even asked people what was going on only to be looked upon as a crazy person. Nobody understood him and he couldn't understand anybody else. When they started boarding the plane, he showed his plane ticket to an airport assistant who waved him towards the plane. He had worried about following the 7 ft giant man, as it seemed he wasn't leaving the departure lounge café. Only at the very last call did the fella board the plane. They did leave nearly an hour late and got to Moscow at the time I had seen on the flight radar. His connecting flight had left Moscow on time. It had failed to show up on radar until 10.50 a.m. because it had to be covered in de-icer. Boarding of the plane had finished on time at 10 a.m. sharp. When he was stood in the X-ray machine with his belt and shoes off they had announced the final call. When he was cleared to enter the departure lounge, he'd had to run to his gate and made it with only a few seconds to spare. As he sat down on the plane, he had worried about his luggage. Had they had time to transfer the bags? When he arrived in Heathrow he found his answer. His luggage had extended its holiday. While talking to my dad I didn't tell him that I had cleaned the kitchen a bit after he left. He's not the superstitious type, but I felt a bit guilty. Perhaps my clearing of dust-bunnies had caused some kind of demonic force to hold on to my dad's suitcase for amusement.

Apocalypse Day came and went without even a hint of the four horsemen. Boris stayed in the mountains, Nataliya Petrovna went about her business and nobody in Russia was hurt. There were no riots, no panic, no fireballs from the sky, and no bullets being fired in the street. The day before the apocalypse was due; I had been summoned to an immigration office to the east of the city near the biggest war memorial. I had to go and collect the new visa that would allow me to leave the country in future. This time there were no would-be-assassins, just a large room with no furniture, and a security guard sat on a windowsill. My visa had already been prepared. The three-month private visa I had entered on was stamped to make it useless, and I was handed a small green booklet with my picture on each page. It looked like an old World War II identity card. I wasn't even charged anything. We left the office and found that the bus we had taken to get there had finished its route in that part of the city, turned around and would be taking us back home. To avoid being asked to give up our seats by babushkas we sat at the back where they never go. The windows of the bus were covered with tiny crystals of ice, so that when car headlights shone through it gave the impression that we were inside a giant Christmas bauble. Sat there, watching the city go by through frosted glass I felt a strange sensation. For days leading up to that moment I had been trying to figure out what I was feeling. I thought it might have been fear. Fear of the cold, or fear of not seeing my family in Wales again for an awfully long time. But I was too relaxed – so it couldn't have been fear. Sat on the back of the bus it felt like I had bunked off school. It was early afternoon and I wasn't normally in the east of the city at that time of day. It reminded me of the time I was in junior school in Ely, and had been picked by a television company to be involved in a few hours' filming for a documentary. I was nine or ten years old. The camera crew took three others and me to Cardiff market, where they wanted us to walk around with clipboards and look like we were carrying out some kind of junior survey. That was the first time I had seen

Cardiff Market. It had felt like an adventure, seeing the market salespeople calling out prices of strawberries and people bartering. I had felt wonderfully free, being away from school and having a taste of adult life. Sat in the giant bauble with my passport and visa in my pocket and Nastya by my side, watching the rays of crystalline light swirl around, I had the sensation that even though I had reached my destination, even though I now had one place to be and would likely be there for years to come, I was at the beginning of my adventure.

EPILOGUE — ONE YEAR
IN SIBERIA & COUNTING

Aeroflot Flight SU1483N. December 25th 2013. Krasnoyarsk — Moscow

Nastya and I both felt excited to leave. Though we had met in Paris, and flown to Moscow together a few times, we had never actually enjoyed a holiday or trip of any kind together as a couple. Thanks to a friend of mine, we had been bumped up to comfort class on Aeroflot's new Boeing 777. Reclining in seats we would never normally be able to afford I looked down on the clouds stretching out into the sunrise. Barely a month had passed since I had celebrated my first full year in Siberia. To mark the occasion I had arranged a small party in a café that doubled as a gig venue and nightclub. I had recently become an English teacher/cultural advisor and so one of my colleagues and several of my students joined us. Without any decent command of the Russian language, it became obvious that teaching would be the only option available to me. It's the perfect job really, as it gives me access to many different people, all of whom are eager to tell their story. It also provides a great deal of insight into the differences that have long existed between the British and Russian ways of life. For instance, while discussing music with one female student in her late thirties, we started on cultural shifts that had happened since the sixties. I talked about all of the music I had grown up with and the famous clash between the mods and the rockers. When I asked her if they had ever experienced any similar kind of musical rivalry in Russia she replied 'No, we had communism.'

Though I couldn't wait to travel, in the back of my mind I had been slightly concerned about flying again. My previous flight had been with my dad over a year earlier, and I distinctly remember a minute where the plane had started falling from the sky after take-off. As was the case a year earlier, the pros outweighed the cons, so I took my fear and placed it beneath my nervous excitement. Something I had become really good at. The days of being too afraid to step out of the apartment or walk down the street alone are long gone too, although I have done away with the soundtrack in my mind so I can listen for people walking too close to me. Regardless of such new vigilance, I still managed to get side blinded by a pack of wild dogs on my way to class in early December. I had been in the middle of the city, in broad daylight at 3 p.m., when a small dog started barking in front of me. As he was only the size of my shoe I thought nothing of it and continued along my way. I failed to notice the two much larger dogs under a fur tree to my right who decided I had walked into their territory. The largest locked its jaws over my right arm. I shook it off and ran. Fortunately, it didn't cause me any harm though my brand new winter coat needed some stitching.

Other than a pack of large furry beasts trying to eat me, as years go it's been mostly pleasant. The summer, though chilly, was full of boat trips up the Yenisei River and festivals on the islands in the city centre, and I even managed to lose my rugby match virginity. Who'd have thought that after thirty years in Wales I would see my first live rugby match in Siberia? While I sat watching players tackle each other, I felt a pang of regret over having never experienced such a thing before, though I was too caught up in the moment for my negative feelings to last. I have little time for regrets these days. I spent most of my twenties looking back at things I didn't do or hadn't done yet. It has taken me so long to realise that I am alive, now, and I can only use the time I have once. I'm not sure when or why this realisation occurred, but it did, and I am now unmistakably different. A year has changed me much. When I'm not working, I attend Russian and German classes. Nastya has queried my decision to learn German several times saying 'It's pointless to learn a language you have no plan to use'; each time I explain how I had wanted to learn languages when I was twenty. I bought phrase books and did nothing with them, because everything I did then was half-hearted. I don't have time for half-hearted attempts anymore. Either I make a decision to do something or I forget about it. I'm not sure whether this is something to do with living in Siberia or whether it comes with age.

Russian Railways Train 258. December 26th 2013. Moscow — St Petersburg

After only one day in Moscow, we were on our way to another city. It had been a hectic first day of travelling. Dropping our luggage off at Masha's, we made a quick visit to Gorky Park before ending up at a café with Evgeny Nikitin. Almost three years had passed since we had last seen each other; before Nastya and I were even married. We had little time. After waking up at no-o'clock in the morning in Krasnoyarsk, flying to Moscow and spending the day on our feet, our eyes were red and conversational skills a little weak. Nikitin and I chatted as if we had seen each other just the day before. The evening vanished and before I knew it we were shaking hands and saying farewell again.

Nastya woke me up the next morning to tell me we couldn't stay another night in Moscow. Masha had relatives coming over; and Olga, Masha's sister who also lived in Moscow, and who had promised Nastya and I that we would be able to stay the night at hers, had withdrawn her offer; the hostels were expensive at short notice, and so there had been nothing for it but to continue on our journey. I barely had time to shower before throwing on my rucksack and heading for the train station. It hadn't changed much, though the ticket office was even harder to find this time as half the station was sectioned off due to some repair work. The place was teaming with thieves just as it had been in 2011. As we were travelling by day and the journey was only ten hours' long, we decided to buy cheap regular seats. This was a mistake. A few hours in and our backs were aching like hell. Not only that but there was a young guy with mad, staring eyes moving round the wagon asking people for their phones, claiming he was too poor to afford one of his own. Later however he seemed to be talking quietly on his own mobile while hunched down in his seat. In the beginning, Nastya and I were worried about going for a cigarette in the section where two wagons join. If we left our luggage Mr Crazy Eyes would likely go through it. As we squirmed in our seats, Nastya overheard the man sitting behind us chatting to someone on his phone. He was militia. We left our luggage and smoked. The day went on like this with nothing to do but sit for a while then go for a cigarette.

Besides the pack of wild dogs in Krasnoyarsk and the guy on the train, I couldn't say that I had encountered any other real dangers throughout my first full year in Russia. However, I can't say the year wasn't without obstacles. For a start, there were and are still major cultural and personal differences between Nastya and I – I would be lying if I said we hadn't fought it out a few times, shouted at each other or cursed under our breath. During the beginning of 2013 we did it rather a lot. It took a good six months to get used to each other's habits. I am and have always been obsessively tidy. Nastya is the exact opposite. When we get up for work in the morning Nastya likes to carpet the floor in clothes before redecorating the kitchen with breadcrumbs. I've had to learn to let things go a lot. When I first moved to Abertridwr at the age of sixteen, although I loved being with my girlfriend and her family, the disorganisation of their house annoyed me. But it was home, and by being homely it was occasionally untidy. It's much the same now. If our apartment looked less messy, I'd probably be equally annoyed because I also hate clinical environments. I've come to live with the fact that homes and places that are lived in, look lived in. It's not mess, it's life. Besides domestic stuff, we have occasionally pissed each other off with other things. For example, Nastya is forever going on about supernatural stuff. She even asked me whether I thought my new coat had attracted the wild dogs to me, because my new coat is purple, and purple attracts evils; though I think the real reason she asked may have more to do with the fact that I didn't buy the blue coat she wanted me to. If something bad happens, Nastya usually blames it on some far-fetched superstitious blah, which causes me to switch my ears off. Then she becomes angry with me for having not listened to a word. In this way, I'm a lot like my dad; I require proof of everything; closing myself off from mysticism and other difficult to explain phenomena. Saying that, in recent years I have experienced a strange sense of synchronicity that I can't explain.

After I met Nastya, whenever I checked my clock, the time was always 14:14, or 12:12, or something similar. I showed my dad back in 2010 – my dad who doesn't believe in anything other than that worms eat you when you die; and then it began happening to him. I took it as a sign that I was in the right place at the right time. It may sound weird but if you checked your watch at random times and it was always some freakish kind of time palindrome you would start to believe in the unusual, wouldn't you? I know that people who have experienced this kind of thing before have been criticised for maybe checking their watch at the exact same time every day, subconsciously. That may have been the case with me. I don't know. What I do know is that I can't explain everything. Just a few years ago, while I was in Cardiff and too lazy or stuck in my ways to even visit friends on the other side of the city, if you had told me I would be living in the centre of Siberia now I probably would have laughed. Still, when Nastya tells me that a distant relative has become pregnant only because some other distant relative has recently died, or that an apocalypse is due because a bird flew into our balcony window, I still tend to zone out.

Tallink Silja. Baltic Princess. December 30th 2013. Turku — Stockholm

Three days in the city of St Petersburg proved more than enough for both of us. By day it seemed that the whole city had been built for cultural tourism. There are more museums than I can count. But by night it was as if the whole city turned into a party. It did not sleep, and neither did we. Even while I was bunkered down in a hostel, I could feel the vibration continue until dawn. When our bus arrived we couldn't wait to leave. Modern St Petersburg requires a lot of energy and we were decidedly past it.

The bus drove all night, through the Russian border and into Helsinki. When we arrived at the main bus terminal at 10 a.m. Nastya spotted an Indian restaurant, made a beeline for it and banged on the door. We could see a woman vacuuming through the window. She alerted a man who then came to the entrance. It was obvious that we had come from Russia and that we were very hungry. Thirty minutes later he opened up early especially for us. Although we had averaged about one café an hour in St Petersburg, that first taste of curry was magic. When the sun set on Helsinki we were off once more, west into Turku, which is where we caught the ferry to Sweden. Sitting up at night, looking at Finnish houses dotted along the coast, I found myself thinking of Baba Ira. She had died on a Tuesday.

Before Ira passed, she would often be found sitting on the floor of her bedroom for no reason. She didn't know why or how she got there and occasionally couldn't remember who anyone was either. I was called over a few times to help lift her back into bed. After that came a short spell in hospital, which only seemed to make her worse. She gave up on food and soon after gave up her will to speak. She died peacefully in her sleep, in the comfort of her own bed, a few days after being released. She was ninety. Two days later, we buried her in a cemetery on the other side of the city, in the same plot as her husband. At her funeral Ira was laid in clothes she had pre-chosen for the occasion long ago, while I sat with many other members of the family and friends as a priest gave a eulogy and burned incense. We were given candles and stood with them in our hands until they burned to nothing. Wax dripped over our fingers, which burned momentarily, though it reminded us that we were still alive and well. At the cemetery Ira's open coffin was placed on a small wooden platform so that everyone could say their last goodbyes. Nastya and I were encouraged to touch her hand. This took the sense of death and sorrow out of the occasion. It was like shaking someone's hand in farewell. Once her coffin had been laid in the ground, and we had each thrown a handful of dry soil on top, we looked on as the young men who had only dug the hole a few hours earlier, filled it in again. We couldn't leave until it was finished, tidied up, and a cross placed on top. Since then we have feasted three times: once on the afternoon of her funeral, the second five days after, and the third and final exactly forty days after her death. As opposed to the tearful wakes I have known in the UK, The Three Feasts of Ira weren't all doom and gloom. We shared memories and toasted her long life. Nastya and I spent a few hours looking through Ira's old photo albums and listening to her cousins tell stories of Ira's youth. Apparently she had been quite adventurous. She would invite people to dinner, only to announce she would be leaving that very evening for some distant part of the world. She loved to be spontaneous and buy plane tickets on a whim. Even though she was married, she sometimes travelled alone. She wanted to see the world and the expectations of women of her time wouldn't stand in her way. When she was alive, the only Ira I knew was the shadow of a woman who crouched over a stool and ate soup twice a day. Since her death I have learned so much more. If anything I regret not learning more about Ira's life from Ira herself, who would have been only too happy to share her memories with me. Inspired by Ira, Nastya and I have found a new sense of urgency. Two weeks after the final remembrance, Nastya bought us plane tickets to Moscow, train tickets to St Petersburg, and ferry tickets to Sweden. Though we never had any reason to travel to Sweden in particular, we couldn't think of one reason not to. Our decision had less to do with the destination than it had to do with rediscovering the feeling that we were making the most of our time.

Aeroflot Flight SU1482E. January 5th 2014. Moscow — Krasnoyarsk

For some reason the plane back to Krasnoyarsk was barely half full. We'd been placed in the centre row, meaning we had four seats to use as our own. Nastya lay across three of them and fell asleep sharpish, leaving me to think about what we were going back to. After six to ten months of living in Siberia, I had felt like I needed to get out and be somewhere else. Then after walking around Sweden for a couple of days Nastya and I couldn't help but miss Siberia. But from the moment we had to leave Stockholm and turn back towards Krasnoyarsk we both felt slightly miserable. We had been spoilt. The streets of both Stockholm and Helsinki were human friendly. The buildings weren't crumbling, the paving was even and had been laid well, there were no metal poles protruding from the ground right in the centre of the pavements, and there were no giant factories billowing smoke out into the sky or packs of wild hounds. As much as I have loved living in Krasnoyarsk, Siberia and Russia, towards the close of 2013 my experience of it was slightly marred.

At the end of June, Russia passed a very vaguely worded law banning the 'propaganda of non-traditional sexual relations'. This was drafted in as some measure to prevent young people from accidentally turning or choosing to be homosexual. Although the measure didn't affect me directly, I found it disturbing that there was a large group of people that I could no longer talk about, and who couldn't talk about themselves without fear of persecution. The law itself is actually aimed at talking to minors about homosexuality, but even talking or writing about 'non-traditional sexual relations' in a positive light anywhere can be construed as propaganda. Therefore I now have to refer to some as 'people I cannot talk about legally without the threat of prosecution (PICTALWTTOP).

After the law was passed, I asked some of my friends in Krasnoyarsk what it meant for them and whether they had any feelings on the subject. Few people were against it. The majority thought the law was necessary, and some even thought it didn't go far enough. These people I now refer to as anti-humans. As far as they're concerned Russia isn't a place for anyone and everyone. There are able-bodied 'traditional' Russians, and then there is everyone else. Consequently, the PICTALWTTOP cannot clearly identify themselves as being so. To avoid the threat of violence they have to mask their sexuality/personality/ identity. It's rare to see openly PICTALWTTOP in Krasnoyarsk, which furthers the view shared by anti-humans, that there are 'no PICTALWTTOP in my city'. I've heard that phrase so many times now. Sometime before Christmas, a friend of mine, a female of middle age, came to me with a bruised face. She had been assaulted by a group of men because she was quite open about her being one of the PICTALWTTOP.

Russian men, for the most part, proclaim to respect women to the '-nth degree' – they help them take their coats off and open doors for them, as if women can't do these things for themselves; it's claimed they have 'an old-fashioned respect for women' – just not women who love women. When I discussed this violent attack with some of my friends, they simply shrugged it off. 'It's what people get for being unnatural' apparently. Unnatural is a term I heard said a lot towards the end of the year. When I asked another anti-human if he/she thought the PICTALWTTOP should be segregated from society to protect the rest of Russia, he/she said 'yes but then the world would cry genocide'. This same person then went on to explain that the Roman Empire had fallen because there were too many PICTALWTTOP, who had weakened the level of masculinity required for Rome to continue its empire.

Most of the anti-humans seem to think that 'non-traditional sexual relations' are something you choose when you're in your teens, if you're exposed to propaganda. Though when I asked one anti-human when he/she chose to be heterosexual, he/she replied that no choice was ever necessary as no one ever spoke of the PICTALWTTOP in Soviet times, and no PICTALWTTOP were ever seen anywhere. The fact that being one of the PICTALWTTOP was an actual criminal offence before 1993 was apparently not worth taking into consideration. Listening to the anti-humans run off their fascist diatribes often turned my stomach. There is such an air of hostility to those who don't conform to 'the ideal', that it would come as no surprise to me if the Russian government announced some sort of removal, or 'cleansing' programme tomorrow.

In Russia, men must be men. They must buy Swiss army knives (which are sold nearly everywhere), they must have a swagger, wear beanie hats, look as if they have big muscles, go fishing, climb mountains; be 'men', or 'men's men' without literally being a man's man. Women on the other hand must look attractive, climb mountains, but climb to a lesser height, wear dresses, keep their figures, and be mothers. There is little or no room for people outside these expectations.

The second thing that negatively affected the magic of living in Krasnoyarsk was the transferral of Pussy Riot member Nadezhda Tolokonnikova from the prison in Mordovia to a prison hospital in Krasnoyarsk. I knew the prison, because I had walked past it on my way to rugby matches. At first I was angry about the transferral, but for all the wrong reasons. Now people would be able to say 'Pussy Riot sent to Siberia', which of course would reinforce the old negative stereotype. And with her detention being in my home city, Krasnoyarsk would therefore only become known in the Western world as 'that place where Pussy Riot were sent to'. I didn't want that, because Krasnoyarsk is so much more than the detention centre. Before this, the Pussy Riot saga had been something far away, outside of Siberia, and therefore something outside of my life. I was able to comfortably distance myself from it, as Siberians are able to feel a distance from Moscow. But then it landed on my doorstep, and what it revealed was that I had less concern about the life of a person, sentenced to two years in prison for singing a protest song, and more concern for the reputation of a city. I had to check myself, because my love for Krasnoyarsk had blinded me to the suffering of others. Although I wasn't actually an anti-human, I couldn't say I was a humanitarian either. It became obvious from then on that Krasnoyarsk and I had become inextricably linked, that I was also undeniably complicit in the detention of a young woman from Moscow. It was a bitter pill to swallow. Thankfully both members of Pussy Riot were released from prison in late December under a new amnesty bill, along with Mikhail Khodorkovsky, the famous oligarch dissident who had been imprisoned back in 2003. Though the amnesty bill was widely seen as a political stunt to make Russia appear more human friendly before the opening of the 2014 Winter Olympics in Sochi, I was still glad of the fact. This time for the right reasons.

I don't want to be seen as someone who condemns Siberia as a backward land; because I'm not, and it isn't. 'People are people, and people have a right to life', is another expression I heard in 2013. And though I heard it less than the anti-human views, it goes to show that there is hope. Though I occasionally like to think that I am more civilised, because I don't believe in regular apocalypse, domovoi, or humans being 'natural' and 'unnatural', I too have been forced to admit that I have my own faults. Both Nastya and Siberia are equally responsible for this realisation of contradictions within myself, and I am a better person because of it.

As the plane began its descent into Krasnoyarsk, my feeling of gloom subsided. I was glad to be getting home. Krasnoyarsk was, after all, the place that granted me amnesty. If it wasn't for Russia, Nastya and I would never have been able to live together, we might never have married and our relationship might have ended back in 2011. Though other people's rights are not recognised in Russia, the right of Nastya and I to be a family had been. This is something I am ever thankful for. Though there is much room for improvement in Russia, there are many things that it gets right, and credit must be given where it is due. If it weren't for Russia, not only would this journal have no reason for being, but my world would be so much smaller. I would be roughly the same person I had been before I left for Moscow in March 2011; because of all the things, people and possessions I left behind in Wales, what I miss the least is me, the 'me' of the past. When I first moved to Siberia, my biggest complaint was that I had to bring myself with me. I thought that the person I was could never be separated from the person I would become, that there would be so many trace elements it would be impossible to be anything other than precisely who I was. For so many years I often dreamt of meeting my past self, and giving him a kick in the arse. I wanted to change the man I used to be so much, because I couldn't admit that I was still that same person. Today, if I were to meet my pre-Siberian self, I would probably have nothing to say to him; nothing at all. For we are strangers now.

Acknowledgements:

Thanks to the archives and staff of one of Moscow's museums, Marina Tsvetaeva; the poetry of Yevgeny Yevtushenko and Aleksandr Solzhenitsyn's *The Gulag Archipelago* – all so useful when researching this book. I also found the following websites invaluable during my fact-finding missions:

bbc.co.uk
independent.co.uk
siberiantimes.com
usinfo.ru
go2add.com
csmonitor.com
armscontrol.org
www.fas.org
state.gov
lonelyplanet.com
stolby.ru
ceuweekly.blogspot.ru
symbolic-mirage.blogspot.co.uk
memorial.krsk.ru
newworldencyclopedia.org
dommuseum.ru
rt.com

theday.co.uk
telegraph.co.uk
russiavotes.org
nytimes.com
forbes.com
metro.us
rferl.org
forbes.com
themoscownews.com
themoscowtimes.com
huffingtonpost.co.uk
theguardian.com
greenpeace.org
bellona.org
washingtonpost.com
projectavalon.net
perezhilton.com

Further Acknowledgements:

For putting me up for the night or acting as a pillow or mattress, I would like to offer my most sincere thanks to Gaz, Alex Werner, Ryan, Brad, Guto, Ed, Mace, Sam, Ruth and Ed's Crocodillo.

For looking at early chapters of this book I would like to thank Peter Brooks, Lynne Rees, Dad and Mali Evans.

For offering support, helping me out in a variety of other ways, and being nice when they could have been otherwise, I'd like to thank the following people and organisations: my mum, my dad, Lindsey and Jon, Siw Hughes, Parthian Books, Meic Birtwhistle of Trefenter, Susan and Etienne Evans of Abertridwr, JJ, Ruth Barnett, Chapter Arts Centre, Aeroflot, especially the pilots who could probably pilot a plane through hell and still land it safely, Russian Immigration, The Russian embassy in London, The British embassy in Moscow, Alun Burge, Alun's neighbours, Evgeny Nikitin, everyone at *Blown Magazine*, Rachel Trezise for telling me 'what not to write', Zoë Brigley, Bill Rees, Katy Evans-Bush, Alan Perry, Jean Perry, Aida Birch, Amanda Birch, Siôn Tomos Owen, Siôn's mum and dad, *The Moscow Times*, *The Siberian Times*, and everyone else who I can't recall.

For giving me a place to sleep on a million occasions, generally saving my neck from ruin and death, and being a decent sort of fella, I offer blokeish manhugs to Torben Schacht. Without you, not only would it have been ten times harder moving to Siberia but I would have no cover for this book.

For their patience and supplying me with five different Russian visas, I offer huge thanks to realrussia.co.uk

I would like to offer extra special thanks to my wife, for being able to read my mind, general love and gooeyness, and inspiration; my mother and father-in-law, for their support, *pelmeni*, and for putting up with my Britishisms, and everyone I have met in Siberia this past year who have helped me forge a new life.

Lastly, I offer the biggest and bestest thanks to editor extraordinaire Susie Wild, for those nights in the Uplands, kicking me in the arse, and turning a pile of notes haphazardly written into... this. Without you, this whatever it is, wouldn't be whatever it is.